How to Write Web Copy and Social Media Content

Spruce up Your Website Copy, Blog Posts & Social Media Content

First Edition

PAUL LIMA

WWW.PAULLIMA.COM/BOOKS

Cover and interior design, Paul Lima

Published by Paul Lima, Toronto, Ontario, Canada www.paullima.com/books

Quantity discounts available for instructors and workshop leaders purchasing class sets. Contact Paul Lima – info@paullima.com.

Library and Archives Canada Cataloguing in Publication

Lima, Paul, 1954–

How to Write Web Copy and Social Media Content: Spruce up your website copy, blog posts and social media content / Paul Lima. – First edition

ISBN 978-1-927710-08-1

Table of Contents

Preface

Welcome to *How to Write Web Copy and Social Media Content*, a book written for those who want to make their website and blog copy sparkle and boost the effectiveness of their social media content, such as tweets and Facebook and LinkedIn posts and participation.

This book is based on business-writing and online and social media copywriting courses that I teach online for University of Toronto continuing education students and for corporate clients and private students. It will help you do the following:

- organize your thoughts before you write
- become a more effective and efficient online writer
- make your points in a clear, concise, easy to read or scan manner
- achieve your purpose and obtain feedback, if so desired

This book is all about communicating more effectively online so your readers understand why you are writing and what action, if any (remember, a "click" is an action), you need them to take. In short, this book will help you write in a more focused and effective manner and simplify your online communications.

When it comes to writing for online media, this book will get you grounded—especially if you feel like you're often spinning your wheels when you write. It will get you thinking about your audience, your purpose, your desired outcome and how to structure your copy or content before you start to write. Then it will help you effectively and efficiently write in a clear, concise, focused manner. You will be introduced to the business-writing process and come to understand the importance of following that process no matter what you are writing.

Paul Lima
www.paullima.com

Chapter 1: Communication Process

Communication is a process. If you want to communicate effectively—in writing (or when speaking)—you should understand the process. Communication requires a sender who sends a message through a channel to a receiver. The process is not complete, however, without feedback; feedback closes the communication loop. Sometimes, noise (competing messages, distractions, misunderstandings) interferes with your message; feedback lets you know if the receiver has received and understood your message.

When you communicate in person, you can ask for feedback: ask people if they understand what you are saying or if they have any questions. However, when you communicate in writing or through other one-way media (such as broadcast), it is more difficult to ask for feedback. Advertisers have learned how to use direct-response marketing techniques such as discount coupons, time-limited offers and so on to motivate and measure feedback.

Advertisers want feedback when they communicate so they can measure the effectiveness of their promotions. If they cannot gauge the effectiveness of promotional campaigns, how will they know whether they should run the same ads again, modify them or scrap them and come up with something new? In business writing, if you do not close the communication loop, how will you know if the desired action has been or will be taken?

Does closing the communication loop mean asking for replies from everybody you email or to whom you send information? Not necessarily. In some instances, your writing purpose might not require you to close the communication loop. You might simply be sending or posting information for the recipient to review—no action required. Alternatively, you might be making suggestions or recommendations that the recipient can act on or ignore.

In other instances, however, you might have to know whether the recipient has taken action or has any questions. If so, you need to close the communication loop. You can somehow follow-up (email or phone, for instance—although not practical in online situations), you can monitor the situation to see if action has been taken or you can close the communication loop and ask for a reply. Again, if you do not require a reply, then you may not need to close the communication loop.

Deciding whether to close it or not should be a conscious decision, however, based on your particular requirements and your writing purpose.

For instance, if you don't care who shows up, or how many people show up, to a meeting or event, then there is no reason to ask people to reply (give you feedback). However, if you need to know how many people will be coming so you can arrange coffee or lunch or the number of chairs you will need, then you had better ask people to let you know if they will be attending. Do you have to give the caterer two days notice to arrange lunch? Then you had better ask people to reply several days before the meeting or event so you have time to notify the caterer.

The important point is this: if you need to know that the receiver has received and understood your message, then you have to put into place a method of closing the communication loop, such as a website address the reader can click on if you are tweeting. If the loop does not close in a timely manner—timely as dictated by you and your circumstances—then it is your job to troubleshoot the process. In other words, you can assume that your message has been received and understood, and that appropriate action has been or will be taken, or you can build feedback into the communication process.

It may seem odd to start a book on online writing with obtaining feedback. However, you often communicate in writing for a reason that usually involves a required, or optional, action. In other words, if you do not know your reason for communicating, if you do not spell out the action you want taken and if you do not close the communication loop, even if it's just a 'click', then you might not achieve your purpose. On the other hand, you might achieve your purpose and not know it because you have not asked the reader to close the communication loop.

With that in mind, where do we begin? How do we tackle this amorphous beast known as writing? I suggest we begin at the beginning, with the writing process—a process that can be applied to any non-fiction writing. However, our focus here will be on online writing.

Chapter 2: Pleased to Meet You

Just as there is a communication process, there is also a writing process. It is a different kind of process. It is the approach you should take before you write, as you are writing and once you have completed writing a document.

If you follow the process, you will become a more effective writer. It's that simple.

You will also become a more efficient writer if you practice following the process. However, as you read the first part of this book, you might find yourself thinking that if you have to follow the writing process every time you write something, especially a short email message or a 140-character tweet, it will take you forever to write anything.

Allow me to ask you this: Would you rather take a little longer to write a document that achieves what you want to achieve or take less time and not achieve your purpose? I presume you would rather do the former. If you do not achieve your purpose when you communicate, you may end up spending more time wondering if your message has been received or sorting out problems or issues caused by mis-communication or ineffective communication. I call that banging your head against the wall.

Most people who follow the writing process find they become more effective writers and, as they practice the process, they also become more efficient writers. This point is worth reinforcing: it takes process-practice to become a more efficient writer; however, following the process will make you a more effective writer from the start.

Again, if you write short email messages or tweets, you may feel skeptical about my "efficiency" claim as you read the first few chapters of this book. Be patient and wait until you come to the five-question writing process shortcut (W5). Again, though, even if following the writing process adds a bit of time to the time it takes you to produce documents, you will become someone who can clearly convey your purpose and desired action so that your readers understand why you are writing and what you expect them to do. I suspect that is something to which every writer aspires.

First introduction

Before you read about the writing process, I want you to take a moment and pretend you are introducing yourself to me. As you will see, I want you to write your introduction three times. To start, I simply want you to write the first introduction however you feel like writing it. Take some time now, before you read on, and write your introduction. I will explain how to write introductions two and three shortly.

Once you have written your first introduction, continue to read.

Writing process overview

Before you write your introduction a second and third time, allow me to introduce you to the foundation of this book: the writing process. The writing process includes five steps. Although all five steps involve writing, in terms of pen on paper or fingers on keyboard, only one step is writing as we view it in the conventional sense of word—constructing sentences and paragraphs. With that in mind, here are the five steps that make up the writing process:

- Preparation

- Research

- Organization

- Writing

- Revision

Again, notice that writing is only one of the steps in the writing process. We will, of course, examine each of these steps in detail. For now, however, I want to focus on why writing is a process and why, when writing, you should follow the five steps in order.

If you are like me, you fear the blank screen or blank page. You look at it and feel intimidated. You see it as an empty vessel you have to fill with words—only you are not sure which words to use, how to order them or how to use all the squiggles (known as punctuation marks) correctly.

Perhaps you are not like me. Perhaps you love the sight of a blank page. You view it as a blank canvas, an opportunity to create. However, you may feel your creations take too long to come to fruition. You start, you stop, you start again. Moving forward is a slow, painful journey, and you often feel you have missed your mark or destination, even if just by a tad, when you are done.

Welcome to the wonderful world of writing.

Writing seems to be painful in some way for almost everyone. For instance, when it comes to spelling and grammar, English is a convoluted and inconsistent language. For many of us, including me, spelling and grammar—let alone stringing words together in coherent sentences—can be frustrating. You can improve your writing, as I have said, and you can write better in less time than it takes you to complete a document today. All you have to do is harness the writing process, which we will discuss in detail later.

Second introduction

I now want you to write your second introduction. This time, we are going to prepare using who, what, where, when and why, known as the W5. Before we look at how you would apply the W5, however, let's look at a few of the things you need to know before you begin to write almost any document:

- word count or page length

- due date

- audience and audience's expectations

- purpose or objective

We know this version of your introduction is due before you complete this chapter, since I am asking you to do it now. You can pretend you are going to send it to me to show me a sample of your writing and to introduce yourself to me. Since it is an introduction, not a website, book or report, it should not be too long.

As your reader or audience, what do you think I need from you? In other words, what is my expectation? Do I want your life history or do I simply want to know who you are and what you do in relation to why you purchased this book? Although the former might be an interesting read, will it be a practical read? The latter, on the other hand, is what you might expect me to want to know.

Finally, what is your purpose in writing your introduction? Let's assume you want to tell me why you bought the book and what you hope to get out of it—how you hope it might help you. With that in mind, I want your second introduction to answer the following questions:

- *Who* are you?

- *What* do you do (or hope to do)?

- *Where* did you buy this book?

- *When* did you buy this book?

- *Why* did you buy this book?

Before you write your second introduction, answer the above questions in point form. Then review your points and determine which ones you would want to use in your introduction. How do you determine that? Think of who I am and who you are, my (the reader's) expectations and your purpose for writing. Eliminate any points that don't make the cut, write your second introduction and revise it as may be required.

Once you have written your second introduction, continue to read.

What did we do?

Consider the writing of your second introduction as an introduction to the writing process. How so? Let's look at what we just did:

1. Preparation

    a. defined the audience

    b. determined the expectations of the reader

    c. defined the writer's purpose

2. Research

    a. conducted internal research by answering the W5 questions

3. Organization

    a. organized the document into a rudimentary outline (when you eliminated points you did not want to cover)

4. Writing (first draft)

5. Revision

The preparation, research and organization should have helped you focus your document on your reader and your purpose, as well as eliminate any points that did not relate to your reader or purpose. Therefore, you should have a more focused and concise document that makes sense to the reader and helps you achieve your purpose. Shouldn't any business document or online writing be both focused and concise? Shouldn't it make sense to the reader and help the writer achieve a predefined purpose?

Third Introduction

So are we done with our introductions? It depends on two things: How long is your introduction and what person did you use? Did you use first person (I, me, my, we, us) or third person (he, she, they)? While correspondence can be in first person, many documents, such as proposals, reports or website copy and blog posts, are often in third person. You could write a message like this: "Based on our second quarter sales, I have decided to give all of my employees a bonus." You are more likely, however, to write a message like this: "Based on second quarter sales, ABC Inc. has decided to give its employees a bonus."

Sometimes the choice of which person to use is subjective. For in-stance, I have used the third person in the "About" section of my website (www.paullima.com) to promote my business writing and business-writing training. Here are a couple of excerpts from the page:

A qualified adult educator, Paul develops and teaches business writing, email writing, report writing, advertising copywriting, media release writing and media interview training seminars for corporate and non-profit clients. He has conducted business writing, copywriting and business of freelance writing courses for adult education students at the University of Toronto, Humber College and George Brown College.

An experienced freelance writer, Paul writes case studies, Web content, media releases, promotional brochures, ad copy and speeches for corporate and non-profit clients. He has written business profiles and articles on the business use of technology for numerous publications, including: *The Globe and Mail, National Post, Toronto Star, Backbone, Profit, Network World Canada* and other print and online publications.

I could go on, but I will not. Why third person, though? Third person helps make the about me statement feel credible; it does not feel like hard sell copy or content. Again, that may be a subjective interpretation. However, the distance of third person can lend objectivity and a greater degree of credibility to a document, as in this case:

After reviewing the results of the recent product awareness survey, ABC Consulting recommends that 123 Ltd. broaden its marketing reach to include adults between the ages of 35 and 45.

By using "ABC Consulting," the document carries more weight. In other words, the company—not just one individual—is making, and there-fore standing behind, this recommendation. Replace "ABC Consulting Inc." with "I" and the statement loses power.

In addition, we often write bios in third person—perhaps to appear on a website or to be read by someone who introduces you before you make a presentation or give a speech. Third person also gives you a sense of distance from yourself. That sense of distance can help you revise your work to ensure it is as focused, complete and concise as it should be.

There are many times, though, when using first person is perfectly acceptable and even preferable. For now, however, I want you to review your second introduction. If it uses first person, I want you to write it one more time, in third person. Even if your bio is already in third person, make sure the length is appropriate for the occasion. Remember, you were asked to introduce yourself to the author of this book. Ask yourself what the author would want to know about you, the buyer of the book, and what you would want the author to know. If your bio is more than five sentences long, reduce it to no more than five sentences. In this way, you will more formally experience revision, the final step in the writing process.

Once you have written your third introduction, continue to read.
If you want to introduce yourself, email your introduction to info@paullima.com.

Chapter 3: Loosening Up

Before we look more formally at the writing process, I want to introduce you to two writing exercises—freefall and directed freefall—that will help you separate the writer from the editor. The writer is your creative self and exists in the right side of your brain. The editor is your logical or linear self and exists in the left side of the brain. Your goal should be to write or create first, and then revise later. In other words, when writing, you want to keep the left and right sides of your brain separated.

If you do not follow the process, you will revise *and* edit when you should be creating. You will waste time proofreading work that is not even at the first draft stage. You will feel inadequate because you are planning instead of writing—as if it were illegal, immoral or unethical to think before you write. In short, if you do not follow the process, your writing will suffer.

Words for thought

Writing is difficult enough without having your internal editor or internal critic to squeeze the last ounce of fun out of what should be a challenging but enjoyable and creative art or craft. With that in mind, chew on a few words for thought:

> Never look at a reference book while doing a first draft. You want to
> write a story? Fine. Put away your dictionary, your encyclopedias, your
> World Almanac and your thesaurus.... You think you might have
> misspelled a word? Okay, so here's your choice: either look it up in the
> dictionary to make sure you have it right—and break your train of
> thought—or spell it phonetically and correct it later. Why not? Do you
> think the word is going to go away? When you sit down to write,
> write. Don't do anything else except go to the bathroom and only do
> that if it absolutely cannot be put off.
>
> – Stephen King, On Writing: A Memoir of the Craft

So what is King saying? When you are writing, you must overcome your internal censor. In short, when you are writing, spelling and grammar do not count. Spelling and grammar are important; however, there will be time for correcting later, once you plan your attack and complete your first draft, which is for your eyes only. In other words, who cares if there are typos? Fix them later.

If you are working in a word processing program such as Word and you have spell checker and grammar checker turned on, you are inviting your internal critic to inhibit your writing. The green and red squiggles under your words, phrases and sentences mean you are seeing (and correcting) so-called mistakes as you write—before you complete your first draft. Every time you revise—when you should be writing—you are wasting time and derailing your train of thought. If you want to improve your writing productivity immediately, turn off spell check and grammar check. Write when you should write; edit/proofread after you have written.

I want to reinforce one point before we move on. *Spelling and grammar are important.* I try my darnedest to catch spelling and grammar mistakes. However, I don't do it while I am writing my first draft. I do it after I have completed what I consider a solid first draft. In fact, before I look for spelling and grammatical mistakes, I edit for big picture items such as tone and content. Then I focus on the more mundane—yet important—task of checking spelling and grammar.

Freefall

I know it can be difficult to separate your editor from your writer. That's why I want to introduce you to a stream of consciousness writing exercise known as freefall.

Freefall is a means of writing whereby you literally write, for five minutes or so, without stopping. When you freefall, you don't have to have anything in particular to write about. You just put pen to paper (recommended over fingers to keyboard) and write, write, write. You don't stop, no matter what. Think of yourself as an artist practicing gesture sketching (rapidly drawing and playing with lines or "gestures" that do not necessarily become pictures).

To sustain your freefall, tap into your stream of consciousness—the thoughts that are flowing through your mind (even as you are reading this page, you can hear them rushing through your mind)—and write, write, write. If you feel yourself coming to a halt, doodle or use ellipsis (...) until you tap back into the stream. Do not stop.

Do not stop to correct spelling, grammar or punctuation.

Do not stop to reflect upon or edit your work.

Do not stop.

It can feel unusual to write when you think you have nothing to say, or to continue to write when you know you have made a spelling or grammatical error. However, the point is to get used to the separation of writer and editor by jumping into the stream and letting the current take you anywhere or nowhere in particular.

What I suggest that you do now is this:

- Sit comfortably where you will not be interrupted for the next while.

- Write for at least five minutes; if you can, set a timer for five minutes.

- Pick up your pen, start with whatever is flowing through your mind, and keep on going.

- Don't stop until your time is up.

If you are not ready to freefall, take a break. But don't put off starting for too long. When you are ready…

…Begin your freefall.

Once you have written a five-minute freefall, continue to read.

I encourage you to do this exercise several times a week to help you loosen up and write quickly. You probably won't freefall when you write your online content, but it's a good exercise to help you loosen up and to help you avoid editing as you write.

Directed freefall

Directed freefall works in a manner similar to freefall but you start with an opening line—something to help kick-start your writing. Once you start, you carry on writing just as with freefall. The opening line sometimes imposes structure on your writing. But not always. Sometimes it inspires. But not always. Sometimes it is a relief to have somewhere to start. Sometimes it makes you feel shackled. The point is to use the first line as a starting point and freefall, no matter how you feel.

So take five minutes or so, and try a directed freefall using the line below. If you are not ready to freefall, take a break. But don't put off starting for too long. When you are ready…

…Begin your directed freefall starting with the following line:

It took a long time to…

Once you have written a five-minute directed freefall, continue to read.

When you have completed your directed freefall, try another line. Use a line of your own to get started or use any of these:

- *I find it frustrating when...*

- *If I've told you once, I've told you a thousand times...*

- *Terry had to reschedule the meeting because...*

The goal is to have fun, to play, to create for the sake of creating. To write without revising because separating the writer from the editor is an important part of the writing process. Off the top, it makes you a more efficient writer if you work diligently to keep the writer and editor separate. Also, as you will see when we get to creating outlines, directed freefall—starting to write with an opening line—is an integral part of becoming a more effective business writer.

Again, as you read this book, use freefall (or directed freefall) to exercise your writing muscles.

Once you have written your second directed freefall, continue to read.

Chapter 4: Writing Process

I'd like to take a more formal look at the writing process. As I have indicated, there are five steps in the writing process:

1. Preparation

2. Research

3. Organization

4. Writing

5. Revision

The time required to complete each step varies depending on the nature of the project. For instance, if you are a subject matter expert, you might not have to spend any time on external research. If you write a particular type of document regularly, you might not have to spend much time on preparation; you might even have a template you fill in each time you write.

When writing short messages, you can prepare, research and organize by answering the W5 questions that I will look in more detail later in this book. Answers to these questions will help you think about your audience and purpose, conduct internal research and generate the points (organization) you want to cover in your message. Once you have put your list of points in order, writing should be as simple as turning the points into sentences. Then you revise as may be required to ensure you are making and supporting your primary point (conveying your purpose), proofread to check spelling and grammar and send or post.

When writing a blog post or website copy, however, you will spend more time preparing, researching and organizing. You might even have to produce a formal outline (an integral component of organization) for your own sake or for approval before you start to write. As you write, you might discover gaps in your knowledge and have to conduct more research and incorporate new material into your outline. When you complete your first draft, you will probably spend time revising to ensure that your writing is as clear, concise and focused as it can be, and that all points covered reinforce your purpose and any action you want the reader to take.

You might have to send your document to a superior or a committee for approval. Your superior or the committee will most likely make suggestions and send it back to you for additional work. That is to be expected and is all part of the process.

Effective and efficient

If you follow the writing process, you will become a more effective *and* efficient writer.

Efficient writers spend time planning (preparation, research and organization) before they write. In addition, they allocate time for editing (revising and proof-reading). This leads to the writing of effective documents, documents that achieve specific and clearly defined purposes.

Less efficient writers tend to spend more time overall on projects even though they spend less time planning. They also edit as they write, which is to say they write, tinker, write, revise, write, correct little errors and so on. This is not a productive way to write and, because less efficient writers don't plan what they want to write, they end up with less satisfactory, or less effective, results.

It may seem ironic to say that you can become more efficient if you spend more time planning. However, the time you invest up front in preparation, research and organization pays dividends when it comes time to write and revise.

Think of writing as a trip. If you plan your trip, you are less likely to get lost and more likely to arrive on time. That does not mean you cannot meander as you travel. You can. However, if you meander and your side trip takes you nowhere, you will find it easier to get back on track because you have a road map or, in the case of writing, a process that includes a detailed outline.

Writing process overview

With that in mind, let's review each component of the five-step writing process. I will help you apply the most significant aspects of the major components as you work your way through this book. In addition, as you read about the writing process, remember that I will provide you with a writing process shortcut for short email messages, tweets and other short online posts. Before you get to the shortcut, however, you need to understand the full process.

Preparation
- establish your primary purpose (why you are writing)

- assess your readers (or audience) and their expectations and awareness of the issue(s) about which you are writing

- determine the detail into which you must go to achieve your purpose

- select the appropriate medium for delivering your words

Research

- determine if research will be internal, external or a combination

- find appropriate sources of information

- take notes and document external sources

Organization

- select an appropriate method of development so that your writing unfolds in a logical manner

- prepare an outline, breaking down your document into manageable chunks

- consider your layout, design and visuals (illustrations, graphs, charts)

Writing

- write from outline point to point, using each point like the opening line in a directed freefall; expand each point into sentences and/or paragraphs

- write with spell check and grammar check turned off

- complete a first draft, or a full section of longer documents (like one page in a full website), before revising

- write the introductions and conclusions of longer documents (reports and proposals) last

Revision

- revise with the reader and subject matter in mind to ensure the tone is appropriate for both

- revise to ensure your document is clear, concise and focused and supports your purpose

- check spelling and grammar

- peer edit if possible

Learning from advertisers

Advertisers get to know their target audience (or target market) intimately before they produce advertisements. They conduct research and produce ads that meet the expectations of a well-defined demographic (gender, age range, income level, education level and so on). Sometimes they hold focus groups to get into the heads of their target market so they can produce ads that meet psychographic expectations. (Psychographics describe consumer groups based on psychological or emotional traits, characteristics or lifestyles.)

While you may not need to know your audience as intimately as someone producing advertising or marketing material does, you can still learn from advertisers, in particular from the headlines they use to capture the attention of their target audiences.

Look at how the following headline clearly defines its target market:

Over 40? Acne Blemishes?

The headline is marketing an acne product for adults. Notice how it cuts through the clutter of all the other acne medication ads out there by clearly defining its target market: If you are under forty, then this ad is not for you; if you are over forty but have a clear complexion, then this ad is not for you; if you are over forty and have acne, then this ad is for you.

There are many other examples that we can use, and they will not all seem to clearly define the target market, but an analysis will demonstrate how they clearly speak to a defined target market—if they are effective headlines.

The headline captures attention by clearly defining or speaking to its target market and creating an expectation in the reader. In the example above, readers expect to find a solution to their acne problems. If the rest of the ad copy does not quickly deliver on the implied promise of a solution (in other words, demonstrate how it will meet the created expectation) it will fail to hold the interest of the reader. If it does not hold the reader's interest, it cannot influence the reader's attitude—to believe the product will work, for instance. In addition, if the ad does not influence the reader's attitude, it cannot motivate the reader to take action—in this instance, to buy the product.

AIAA: attention, interest, attitude, action

You may not think you are *selling* when you write but if you want your reader to take a specific action, you need to sell the reader. To do that, you need to do what advertisers do:

- **Attention**: capture the attention of your reader and set expectations

- **Interest**: hold reader's interest by demonstrating how you will meet relevant expectations

- **Attitude**: change or influence your reader's attitude

- **Action**: call for specific action

Depending on what you are writing, you AIAA, so to speak, by doing the following:

- Capture your reader's attention by using appropriate subject lines, titles and sub-titles, opening paragraphs and/or executive summaries.

- Hold your reader's interest with clear, concise, focused writing that reinforces the reader's beliefs and expectations or enlightens the reader through the presentation of relevant information.

- Influence or change your reader's attitude by overcoming any objections your reader might have, informing the reader of the benefits of your position, by stating your case in a logical, persuasive manner—supporting your arguments with relevant facts and/or by building trust in you, your position, your company.

- Achieve your purpose by, if required, defining the action you want your reader to take and asking your reader to take it by a specific date.

In summary, to be an effective business writer, you must AIAA so you can sell your purpose—the reason you are writing—and any action you want the reader to take. Again, you may not believe that you are in sales, however, if you want somebody to do something, you have to sell that person on the action you want taken.

The action might be as complex as recommending that a new highway be built through an ecologically sensitive area or it might be something as simple as asking the reader to click on a link or attend a meeting. The point is, if you don't catch the person's attention, he will not read your message. If you don't hold the reader's interest, he will stop reading and not understand what you want done. If you don't influence attitude, the reader will not be motivated to do what you've requested. In addition, if you do not clearly ask for the sale—or the action—you might not get what you want, when or where you want it.

Before we become more effective writers (and, I hope, more efficient ones too), however, we have to get organized. Let's start with a brainstorming technique known as clustering that will help you conduct internal research and will help facilitate the outlining or organizing process.

Chapter 5: Clustering/Brainstorming

I am now going to introduce you to clustering, a form of word association or brainstorming. Clustering helps you conduct internal research—after you have completed any required external research—before you outline (organize) your document.

Clustering enables you to put on paper all you know about and associate with a topic. It helps you get your knowledge out in the open and helps you reduce the time you might otherwise spend pondering a topic. It also sparks writing ideas because, as you cluster, your mind makes associations and produces images that it would not have otherwise produced. These ideas and associations can help enrich your writing.

When clustering, you follow a specific process in which you quickly jot down all the words and phrases that you associate with a given topic, keyword or phrase. Once you have completed the clustering process, you will find it much easier to produce a formal document outline; having a formal document outline helps you write in a more effective and efficient manner.

Since a picture is worth a thousand words, allow me to show you an example of clustering before I describe how to engage in this activity. What you see in the clustering illustration might look like a messy web of words and phrases. However, it is also gold—internal research and outline gold. To organize your document, and to become a more effective and efficient writer, you just have to learn how to mine the gold from your cluster of words and phrases.

Be open to whatever comes up

When you engage in clustering, you produce words and phrases associated with your subject. You also may produce words and phrases that are only vaguely (or not at all) related. That's not a problem. Just as you do not censor yourself when you are freefalling, you do not censor yourself when you are clustering.

Sometimes jotting down unrelated words that may enter your mind when clustering can lead to jotting down related words and phrases. In other words, there are times when the mind moves in mysterious ways. Let it.

Clustering: how to do it

When clustering, you follow a specific process in which you quickly jot down the words and phrases you associate with a given topic, keyword or phrase. Once you are given (or decide upon) your keyword or phrase, you follow these steps:

1. Jot down the keyword on a blank page; underline and circle it.

2. Moving quickly, draw a dash from your keyword and jot down the first word or phrase that comes to mind; circle that word or phrase.

3. Draw a dash from that word and jot down the next word or phrase that comes to mind.

4. Repeat until you come to the end of your word association string (you will feel this instinctively as you find yourself going blank).

5. Return to your keyword.

6. Moving quickly, draw a dash from your keyword and jot down the next word or phrase that comes to mind; circle that word or phrase.

7. Draw a dash from that word or phrase and jot down the next word or phrase that comes to mind; circle that word or phrase.

8. Follow the clustering process until you feel a natural end to your cluster. You may have on your page two or three strings of words; you may have twenty-two or more word association strings. There is no right or wrong number. The key is to move quickly using the lines and circles to help spark the creative side of your brain.

I generally find it easiest to use a pen and a piece of paper when clustering, or perhaps a white board or flip chart if I'm brainstorming with a colleague or committee. On the other hand, if you are comfortable using computers, there are a number of clustering applications available: Inspiration is one of the more venerable "visual thinking" applications but similar applications are available.

Clustering exercise

Before you complete this first clustering exercise, read the above instructions again. Once you are ready, write down the keyword below and start to cluster. When you are ready, begin clustering using this keyword:

HEART

Once you have completed your cluster, continue to read.

Another clustering exercise

Some people take to clustering. Some people find it difficult to cluster freely. Clustering will prove to be particularly useful when you are writing longer documents. If you find it difficult, allow me to assure you that you will get better with practice. With that in mind, try one more clustering exercise.

Once you are ready, begin clustering using this keyword:

APPLE PIE

Once you have completed your cluster, continue to read.

Applying clustering

Do you have a sense of how clustering can help you conduct internal research or produce an outline? Perhaps not yet, as the above words may not mean all that much to you. In addition, you have no sense of audience or purpose. At this point, however, you should have two pages full of words or phrases that you associate with *heart* and *apple pie*.

Imagine if you were writing about *heart* or *apple pie* and that you had an audience and a purpose in mind. You would most likely have on paper all that you associated with *heart* and *apple pie* in relation to your audience and purpose. (You might also have words and phrases that don't quite relate to *heart* and *apple pie* or to your audience and purpose but sometimes you have to jot down irrelevant information to get to the relevant material.)

If you had a purpose and audience, you would complete *heart* or *apple pie* research before you clustered. Once you clustered your keyword, you would then review the word association strings you produced and separate wheat from chaff— literally highlight words and phrases (topics) that you wanted to cover in your document. From that, as we shall see, you would produce your formal outline.

Allow me to quote an accountant who was taking a business-writing seminar in which I introduced clustering. He had chosen to cluster a keyword that he associated with a major report he was writing for his firm. After completing his clustering, he said:

> You freed one gigabyte of RAM. I was holding it all in and you had me pull this information out of nowhere. Everything I need to know is down on paper. Now that I know what I'm going to say, I have brainpower left to think about how I'm going to say it. It's all over but the writing, and the writing is no longer intimidating.

He said this before moving from clustering to creating an outline. In other words, he saw in his spider's web of words everything he needed to write about and he saw how he could start to organize the information.

Yet another clustering exercise

I know I said you should conduct your clustering after you had concluded any required external research; however, it does not hurt to use clustering as soon as you have a subject to write about because it can help you figure out what you know, and what you need to know, about the subject. Once you have completed your clustering, you do your research. Then, once you have completed your research, you cluster again to help you organize your thoughts. But I digress.

I now want you to think of a keyword or phrase that you associate with an email message, website page, blog post, post you want to use on Facebook or LinkedIn, a tweet or series of tweets you want to write or some other business document. (If you are not working on anything right now, think of a something that you have previously worked on.) Ideally, you want to pick a subject about which you have already conducted some research or about which you have extensive knowledge. However, if you have a new assignment and want to discover what you know and think about it, use the new assignment as your keyword.

The keyword or phrase should be something that defines or summarizes the subject. Once you have that keyword or phrase in mind, write it down, underline it, circle it and start clustering.

Once you are ready, begin clustering using this keyword:

\<Your Keyword\>

Once you have completed your cluster, continue to read.

What now?

Once you have finished clustering, here's what you do:

- Use a highlighter and highlight any words and phrases (topics) that you think you should write about in your document.

- Place the topic words or phrases in priority sequence (the order in which you think you should write about them) to produce a rough outline of your document.

- Review your draft outline and revise it as required based on your subject, purpose and audience. Also keep in mind the scope of the document—short email message versus website copy or blog post or tweets, for instance. As you revise it, eliminate any points you don't need to cover and fill in any gaps with new points you might think of.

In the next chapter, we will look at how to create a formal outline. However, I hope you can see how clustering can draw information out, and how producing an outline based on your clustering means that you don't have to start writing with a blank page. Instead, you can start with an outline, which is kind of like having a series of directed freefall opening lines. To write your document, you simply freefall from outline point to outline point. The more detailed your outline, the less you have to hold on to as you write, and the more effectively and efficiently you will be able to write.

Chapter 6: Creating Outlines

Clustering is the first step in getting organized. The next step is to create an outline. Producing an outline before you write will help you write in a more effective and efficient manner. In addition, if you are wondering why you have to go through all of this to write a simple email message or tweet, stick with me. I am showing you the full, formal writing process now. I will soon show you a writing process shortcut that you can apply to shorter messages.

To create an outline after clustering, you have to move from right-brain (creative) thinking to left-brain (linear) thinking.

After clustering, as I mentioned, take a highlighter to your spider's web of words and highlight any words and phrases that you want to write about in your document. Remember, at this point, you have already thought about your topic, audience and purpose (we will examine purpose in detail later), so you should have a good sense of who you are writing for and why you are writing. Therefore, you can highlight words and phrases that relate to your subject matter, audience and purpose.

Once you have highlighted appropriate words and phrases, you place them in a list to create a rough outline of your document. You review and revise it—put the topics in the order you think you should write about them. Again, this is based on your purpose, audience and scope (the degree of detail expected by your audience or required to achieve your purpose). Also, you consider the deliverable (website page, full website, blog post or series of posts, social media content, email, letter, report, PowerPoint presentation and so on) that you are producing.

Review your ordered list and do some infilling by adding any other topic points or subtopic points, you feel may be missing. Remove any points that are not relevant to your document and you are almost done.

Why create an outline?

Does this feel like work? Most people think it does and there is a valid reason for the feeling. It is work. But what's the alternative? You can, of course, try to fill the blank page with sentences. However, guess what happens when you try to do that? Your brain tries to write well—to write coherent, well-constructed sentences and paragraphs produced in a logical order—and to spell correctly and follow the rules of grammar. As it is trying to do all of that, it tries to keep track of what you have written, what you are writing and what you still need to write.

Now your brain is a remarkable organ; it can do all of that, more or less. What I am suggesting you do here is relieve your brain of some of this workload by creating an outline—a formal list of all the points you need to cover placed in the order you feel you should write about them. An outline brings focus and logical order to your document. It liberates your brain and lets you concentrate on writing each point in a clear, concise manner. Your brain won't have to remember what you have written while thinking about what you are writing and what you still have to write. If you follow the writing process, which lists editing as the final component, you also free your brain from thinking about grammar and spelling on the first draft.

With all this liberated brainpower available, you can focus on making your writing as effective as possible. Isn't that your primary goal—to write as effectively as possible?

Creating outlines

Once you have your points on the computer screen in logical order, you convert them into more detailed points and create your outline. Below are a couple of outline examples. The first is a major topic outline on the subject of creating outlines. The second is a more detailed outline on the same topic. The major topic outline includes the subject you are going to write about and, in this case, sets out the two major topics you are going to cover. It could also be the various pages of your website. Here is our outline:

Creating outlines

1. How to create an outline
2. Benefits of outlining

To create a more detailed outline, you would add sub-points (from your cluster) below the major topic headings, as in the following example:

Creating outlines

1. How to create an outline

    a. outline major topic points

      b.   subdivide topic headings where appropriate

      c.   further subdivide subcategories if appropriate

2. Benefits of outlining

      a.   provides logical structure

      b.   helps you detect errors in logic

      c.   gives you a detailed road map

      d.   lets you meander, if you wish, without getting lost

      e.   removes the stress of trying to hold onto all you know about a topic while you are writing about it

      f.   makes you a more confident writer

      g.   ensures all major and minor points are covered, in logical order

      h.   produces greater clarity and focus

      i.   allows you to write quickly in manageable chunks

      j.   ensures you do not lose your train of thought when you have to take breaks from writing; give examples

      k.   facilitates the approval process, if approval is required

      l.   lets you write from an approved outline

      m.   *should* minimize revisions by superiors

Benefits of outlines expanded

Can your outlines be even more detailed? Absolutely. The greater the scope of the document (in other words, the longer the document), the longer and more detailed the outline should be. I'll show you a longer outline shortly; however, first let me address some of the points listed under "Benefits of outlining" in the outline above.

Outlines provide a logical structure to your document. If you have brainstormed all the points you need to know and listed them in the order that you want to write about them, then you can detect errors in logic. I don't know about you but I'd rather revise a series of outline points before I start to write than revise an entire report several times because my writing did not flow in a logical manner.

In addition, if you have a detailed road map to follow, it will get you from point A to point B in the shortest possible time. Instead of weaving all over the writing road and heading down dead ends, you'll start where you should start, take the route you need to take and end up where you want to be. (Notice how that last sentence was not in my "benefits" outline. But notice how it is related to and logically follows the "gives you a detailed road map" point. That is the kind of focused writing that an outline can help you produce.)

Does that mean you cannot meander? Of course not. If you think of a point that did not make it into your outline, you are free to explore it. If it is something you should write about, make room in the outline for it. If it is something that proves to be a dead-end, leave it out. The point is, even if you wander, the outline will ensure that you don't get lost. It will keep you on track, ensuring that you cover all major and minor points, in an order that makes sense to you, to your topic and to your reader.

A detailed outline means you do not have to hold on to all you know about a topic while you are writing about it. That removes a great deal of the stress that you might otherwise feel while you are writing and helps you write with greater confidence. If you are covering all the major and minor points you need to cover to convey your purpose or achieve your goal, then you will write with greater clarity and focus.

With an outline in place, you can write quickly in manageable chunks. Instead of having to write a fifteen-page website or report, you only have to write a series of pages, chunks or sections. That also reduces the stress associated with writing. In addition, it ensures you do not lose your train of thought when you have to take breaks from writing longer documents. For instance, if the phone rings, you can finish a sentence, take the call and then pick up your writing at the next outline point. Or you can go home at the end of the day knowing you will come back to the document the next day and pick up where you left off—because the next point you want to address is there in your outline.

If you have to get a website or any major document approved before you can go live or distribute it, send the outline out for approval first. The person who has to approve the document can see if you have covered in your outline all the points you need to make. If any points are missing, or if the approver does not think your points are as logically structured as they should be, then he or she can add (or delete) points or move them around before sending the outline back to you. When you start to write, you will be writing to an approved outline.

That does not mean the person who has to approve the document won't make some changes; however, the changes are more likely to be of a subjective nature rather than a request to revamp and reorganize your entire document. I know, however, that some people who have to approve documents will ask you to revamp or reorganize anything you've written, even if you have carefully followed the approved outline. That's why I had points that said "*facilitates* the approval process" not "*guarantees* the approval" and "*should* minimize revisions by superiors" not "*will* minimize revisions…"

Even longer outlines

As I have said, if you are writing a long document, like an entire website, you will want to produce a detailed outline, such as an outline for each page of the website. I'd suggest that you divide your outline into major sections, such as each page (or chapters if writing a book). Beyond that, the premise is the same: outline major and minor topic points. Be as detailed as possible because the time you invest up front, producing a detailed outline, will save you writing (and even revising) time.

In short, a section outline might look something like this:

Major topic of page

1. Major point 1

   a. sub-point 1

   b. sub-point 2

      i. secondary point 1

      ii. secondary point 2

2. Major point 2

   a. sub-point 1

      i. secondary point 1

      ii. secondary point 2

   b. sub-point 2

   c. sub-point 3

      i. secondary point 1

3. Major point 3

    a. sub-point 1

        i. secondary point 1

    b. sub-point 2

        i. secondary point 1

        ii. secondary point 2

You outline every page you want to include in the website and every point you want to make on every page, before you write. You do this in large part by using clustering to determine the various pages of your website (major topics) and the points that belong on each page. This, or course, is done with what your audience needs to know in mind. In short, following the formal outline process will get you to the stage where it is all over but the writing, from outline point to outline point. As any professional writer will tell you, that's a great place to be; however, you don't have to be a professional writer to get to that place.

Outlines in Word

From short messages to long websites, outlines are the key to effective writing. Set up properly, they help you focus on all you have to write to meet the expectations of your readers and achieve your purpose. Acknowledging their importance, Microsoft Word and most other major word processing applications have outline views.

A detailed discussion about Word's outline view goes beyond the scope of this book; however, if you are not familiar with outline view, consider learning how to use it. Outline view lets you create a detailed outline. In addition, once you've completed your outline, you can move from outline view to print layout view and start writing from outline point to outline point.

Having said that, if you are not comfortable with Word's outline view, don't let technology interfere with the creation of your outline. Use clustering to discover the words and phrases you associate with your topic, and create your initial outline using pen and paper. Transfer your initial outline into a normal Word page view. Arrange your outline points so that they flow in the most logical order possible. Then write your document from outline point to outline point.

Clustering/outline exercise

Think of another word or phrase that you associate with an email message, website, blog post, post you want to use on Facebook or LinkedIn, a tweet or series of tweets you want to write or some other business document—or reuse the word or phrase you used previously. Once you have your word or phrase in mind, and are ready, begin clustering using

<Your Keyword>

Once you have completed your cluster, continue to read.

Now that you have completed your clustering, try to produce as detailed and formal an outline as possible based on the outline examples presented in this chapter. With that in mind, here's what you do:

- Take a highlighter to your web of words and highlight any words and phrases (topics) that you think you should write about in your document.

- Jot down major topic or pager or section topic lines, such as "benefits of outlines."

- Below your major topics, place any subtopic words or phrases in sequence (the order in which you think you will write about them) to produce a rough outline of your document.

- Expand your words and phrase to create full points.

- Add any additional related points and subtopic points. (In most instances, you will find them in your clustering. However, sometimes the act of moving from clustering to outline jogs your memory and helps you discover other points.)

- Review your draft outline and revise it as required based on your purpose, audience and project scope; delete any irrelevant points; and fill in any other gaps between outline points with topics that come to mind as you review your outline.

Once you have completed your outline, continue to read.

If you are so inclined, you can try to write based on your outline. Treat each outline point and sub-point as the opening line of a directed freefall, and write from point to point. You don't have to write as quickly as you do when you freefall but try to resist the urge to revise as you write. In other words, keep your writer separate from your editor.

If you are in the mood to read, however, carry on. As promised, we will look at shortcuts that will help you prepare, research and outline short documents such as tweets and email messages.

Chapter 7: Writing Email Messages

I want to take a moment to show you the W5 email-writing shortcut. You can apply the W5 to almost anything you write, but more on that later.

When using the W5, you still follow the writing process—that's crucial to becoming an effective writer. By answering the W5—who, what, where, when and why (and sometimes hoW, making it a W6) you will, however, shortcut the process.

W5 preparation, research and organization

When writing short documents—such as email messages or tweets—and when you do not have to do any, or much, external research, you can reduce the first three steps of the writing process—preparation, research and organization—to a few minutes using the W5 method. You then write your message, edit it as may be required and click send.

W5 is the foundation of journalism. Answers to the W5 are used to outline the lead or opening paragraph of any news article. Journalists, in fact, will tell you they do not start writing any article until they have answers to the W5 in place. There are times journalists find multiple W5 elements (I'll include multiple W5 questions in the email writing exercises), or need more than the basic W5 points, before they can write stories. There are times when they do not use all the W5 points they find. Either way, W5 is the place to start. I am suggesting that W5 should be the foundation of all business writing, especially short messages.

W5 news article outline

Let's see W5 in action. Review the following W5 news article outline:

- **Who**? Russians
- **What**? Held impromptu memorial services; killed 39 people and stirred fears of a revival of terrorism here
- **Where**? At two subway stations in Moscow
- **When**? On Tuesday; brazen attacks a day earlier
- **Why**? Suicide bombers conducted brazen attacks

From this W5 comes the article lead in *The New York Times*, March 30, 2010:

Russians held impromptu memorial services on Tuesday at two subway stations in Moscow where suicide bombers conducted brazen attacks a day earlier that killed 39 people and stirred fears of a revival of terrorism here.

Of course, the full article expands on the W5 and quotes various sources; however, once you have the W5, you have the foundation of the story. Sometimes, once you have the W5, you have the entire story. So the W5 can be the foundation of anything you write and, at times, your W5 can be all you need to write about.

Applying W5 to email

When it comes to writing email, answering the W5 questions can often replace much of the writing process. If you are writing a long or complex document, I suggest you go through the entire writing process before you answer the W5 questions. For most email messages (and tweets as will see on in the chapter on social media), however, answering the W5 questions is all you need to do to focus on your purpose, audience and topic, as well as ascertain what you need by way of feedback, action or reply—if anything.

Answering the W5 questions allows you to think about these points:

- Who: your audience and your audience's relation to you
- What: your topic or subject
- Why: your purpose
- What: details reader requires to understand your topic and purpose
- When and where and event is taking place
- What, when, where (and perhaps how) any action, feedback or reply should take place

By tossing how into the mix you can determine if you need to give the reader explicit instructions concerning any action you require.

Once you've answered the W5 questions, you can take these steps:

- review your answers and decide what you will include and what you will exclude when writing your message

- arrange your points in the order in which you should address them—your formal outline

- write from point to point

- revise as may be required

- hit send

In short, answering the W5 questions lets you prepare, conduct internal research and organize your thoughts before you write.

What are readers looking for?

As you go through the writing process or answer the W5, I suggest that you do it in a reader-centric manner. When writing, you try to achieve your purpose. At the same time, you should think about what your readers are looking for and expecting. What your readers would be looking for is probably the same thing you would be looking for when you receive an email message. Readers would be looking for the following elements:

- a subject line that captures their attention

- your purpose, clearly stated in the opening paragraph: what the message is about and why it is being written

- a well-organized, clear, concise, focused piece of writing that maintains interest (is related to your purpose)

- a message length that is appropriate for the topic and purpose of the message; in email, most messages are one to five paragraphs in length

- a closing paragraph that lets readers know if any action is required; if so, who takes it, by when, where and possibly how

- proper tone in relation to the message and your audience

All of this comes from preparation, research and organization. Or, in the case of email, from answering your W5 questions before you write. With that in mind, let's go through the W5 process for several email messages and do some writing. There are some sample email messages in Appendix One at the back of the book; however, try the exercises below before you read the sample messages.

The thank you note

I'd like you to think of someone to whom you owe a thank you note or whom you would like to thank for a personal or business kindness. Before you do the exercise, make sure you have the name of the person in mind and that you know what that person did to earn your thanks.

Once you are ready, write point form answers to the questions below on a sheet of paper or in a word processing file. I've included multiple W5 questions, most likely more than you'd ask if you were to do this on your own but I want to take you through the full writing process, including what to leave in and what to leave out, before you write (when organizing the points you want to make). With that in mind, answer the questions:

- Whom do you want to thank? (Name the person and note that person's relationship to you.)

- What did that person do; what action did that person take?

- Where did it take place?

- When did it take place?

- What benefit did you derive from the action?

- What was your primary feeling or emotion?

- Why do you want to thank him or her?

- What overt action, if any, do you want the recipient to take upon reading your email? When and where should it take place?

- Should (how should) the recipient let you know she is taking it?

- What covert action (also known as your hidden agenda), if any, do you hope might take place?

Once you have answered the W5 questions, continue to read.

Before we move on, let's examine that last question. Remember all those thank you notes that you sent to your grandparents when you were a child? You sent them after receiving birthday or other holiday-related or special-occasion gifts from them. Although you were truly grateful (or so your parents told you), you probably resisted writing the note—until your parents told you that you might not receive more gifts unless you sent a thank you note. So your hidden agenda was to receive more gifts. However, you didn't say that in your thank you note, did you?

Hidden agendas happen in business too. So before you write anything, you should know what action you want to take place, if anything, and if there are any deeper reasons for writing. You do not necessarily have to address those deeper reasons but you should be aware of them; that awareness will help you strike the right tone in your message.

You probably think you can write a simple thank you note without answering the W5 questions first. You most likely can. What I want you to know is that your brain is going to try to answer the questions regardless, with or without your active participation. It is ineffective, however, to have your brain thinking about answers to those questions as you are writing.

Just as you need to separate the writer from the editor, you want to separate the planner/researcher from the writer. Obviously, the more complex the message you are writing, the more important it is that you do so. I am asking you to start the separation process here, with a simple message, so you can learn how to do it. Then do it whenever you write, so you can develop the separation habit.

What you did when answering the W5

When you answered the above W5 questions, you started to go through the writing process. Specifically, here is what you did:

- prepared by establishing your primary purpose: why you were writing, what actions, if any, you wanted to see occur

- assessed your audience: who they were, what they did, where and when it happened

- determined the details to be included in the note: how you felt, what benefit you derived, what action you wanted the reader to take

- conducted internal research using your memory as the source of information

After jotting down point-form notes in answer to the questions, you are almost organized. You probably have more information than you want to use in your final email message. Part of getting organized, however, is deciding what to include and what to exclude. In fact, many writers will tell you that having more information than you need to use is a good place to be because it lets you think about what you need to say and don't need to say, which helps you focus.

If you are working on paper, highlight the points that you want to address in your thank you note. Once you have completed your highlighting, transfer your points to a word processing document. If you are working on your computer, save your research and create a new file. Copy and paste your research into the new file and delete any points you don't have to express. (Save your original research in case you delete material that you later decide you need. This way, you will have it handy rather than having to recreate it.)

Decide where you are going to start but keep in mind that readers want to know why (your purpose) you are writing. You might then recreate the event, describe your feelings or detail the benefits you have derived. It's your choice. The one thing you want to do, though, is get to your purpose—"thank you"—in that first paragraph. After all, your purpose is to thank your reader, so don't wait until the end of your message to achieve your purpose.

Once you jot down a purpose point, jot down all the other points you want to make (based on your W5 answers). Remember, you get to decide what to leave in and what to leave out. Once you have done that, arrange them in the order in which you would logically address them. With that, you have prepared an outline so that your writing will unfold in a focused, logical manner.

Write and then revise

Since this is a short thank you note, you do not have to consider layout or design. You can simply write from outline point to outline point, expanding each point into sentences. Write with spell check and grammar check turned off.

When you are ready, write your thank you note based on your W5 outline.

Once you have written your thank you note, continue to read.

Once you have completed the first draft of your thank you note, review your sentences and/or paragraphs. Ensure that each paragraph contains no more than one significant point or ensure that the points contained in each paragraph are directly related to each other. (See Chapter 20: Constructing Paragraphs.) Revise with your reader, topic and purpose in mind. Ensure that the tone is appropriate to the subject and that your document is clear, concise and focused, and supports your purpose. Then check spelling and grammar.

Finally, if this is an email, add a subject line. Think of your subject line as an attention-grabbing headline. But remember, the subject line does not have to be in-your-face to grab attention. It should be tone appropriate and pique the curiosity of the recipient by stating your purpose or at least alluding to it.

It is possible, even probable, that the entire process took longer than it would have taken you to just sit down and write the thank you note off the top of your head. I hope, though, that the note you have written is as effective, if not more effective, than the note you would have written had you just started with the blank screen. In addition, the more you practice this process, the less time it will take to prepare, research and outline your short messages before writing them.

The more prepared you are, the more complete your research is and the more detailed your outline is, the less time you will spend writing. That makes you more efficient.

The more prepared you are, the more complete your research is, the more detailed the outline is, the clearer and more concise and focused your writing will be. That makes you more effective. The clearer, more concise and focused your writing is, the less time you will spend revising—and the time you do spend revising will be more productive. But none of this will happen magically. It will only happen if you practice the five-step writing process repeatedly.

As mentioned, there are some sample email messages, including thank you notes, in Appendix One for you to review.

Now let's try one other messages—a complaint.

The complaint email

Let's complain or at least ask that a situation be rectified. You choose the topic:

- Did you have problems obtaining this book?

- Are you currently dealing with a problem with a superior, subordinate or peer at work?

- Are you having any work-related problems that are irking you?

- Have you had problems at a retail outlet or with a product or service?

- Are you having problems with City Hall or any other level of government?

- Are you having problems with a spouse, partner or child?

- Is there any other problem you would like to try to rectify?

Sometimes, when you want to complain or want a situation to be rectified, especially if you've been battling for ages, you have to write a longer message. You also might find negative emotion or feelings creeping into your email. In this particular exercise, I want you to keep your message as appropriately short, succinct and positive (constructive or reasonable, you might say) as possible.

With that in mind, focus on the complaint or situation you want rectified and answer the following questions:

- To whom are you writing? What is your relationship?

- Why are you writing?

- What are you complaining about or what do you want rectified?

- Where did this take place?

- When did this take place?

- Why did this take place?

- What is your primary feeling or emotion?

- Why do you want a resolution?

- What action would it take to satisfy you?

- When, where and how should this be done?

- Did you previously complain to this person about this situation? If so, where and when? With what result?

- What action will you take if the situation is not resolved?

Follow the thank you note process and write. Don't forget to delete any points you don't need to include in your message once you create your initial outline. The goal is to have on paper only the points you want to address, in the order you should address them. Also, ensure your purpose is clear and up front in your subject line and opening sentence or paragraph. Revise as may be required and you are done.

Once you have written your complaint note, continue to read.

Final email exercise

Before you look at the sample email messages in Appendix One, take some time and complete one more email writing exercise. For this final exercise, I'd like you to write a business or work-related email message. Feel free to come up with your own idea for this email message; however, if you need an idea, here are some suggestions you can choose from:

- arrange a meeting
- solicit a quote
- query a tardy supplier
- request an overdue payment
- report on progress to a colleague, supplier, vendor
- request assistance on a project
- request required information

Before you write, come up with the W5 questions you want to answer to help you think about your reader, conduct internal research and organize your thoughts. Doing these tasks first will help you focus your writing. If your writing is focused (follows a thoughtful outline), you should spend less time revising. You will still revise but you will be revising a solid first draft. If you feel you need a bit of help writing sentences and paragraphs, take a peek at Chapters 19 and 20 (Writing Sentences and Constructing Paragraphs) in the book.

Once you have written your work-related note, continue to read.

Chapter 8: More on W5

Talk, talk, talk. But we haven't written one online word yet. Or have we? I am suggesting that you think before you write anything. Do you have to freefall? Will you always cluster? Do you have to follow the full writing process? Do you have to create an outline, let alone a detailed one?

It depends.

How complex a document are you trying to produce? I doubt that you will freefall or create a detailed outline before you write a 140-character tweet. At the same time, as we saw with writing email messages, thinking before you write can lead to a more effective missive. I am here to say it can lead to more effective writing overall, even tweets.

Who are you writing? Why are you writing them? What are you writing about? What action do you want them to take? When and where should they take it? When and where is the what you are writing about taking place?

That is the minimum thinking you should do. If you are going to write a blog post, a series of tweets, a full website or several web pages, ask the W5. At the same time, the longer the document, the more you should cluster your topic and outline what you want to write before you write it.

But let's look at the W5 in more detail for a moment.

As mentioned, journalists use the W5 to write news article leads. And I am suggesting you can use it too—or the appropriate aspects of it—when writing website copy, blog posts, tweets and other social media content.

If you want to quickly grab your reader by the lapels (capture their attention) and hold on to their interest, I suggest you start with the W5 lead or opening. If you are producing a blog where people are going to hang out and read in a leisurely manner, you can get away with what is known as a soft lead. But that kind of online writing is the exception, not the rule.

Let's look at several sample news or W5 leads. Here is a W5 news lead:

Lead: International Business Machines chairman and chief executive Louis Gerstner will face a friendlier group of shareholders at the annual meeting in Toronto today, after the computer giant last week posted surprisingly strong earnings for the last quarter.

Let's deconstruct the W5:

- **Who**? International Business Machines chairman and chief executive Louis Gerstner

- **What**? will face a friendlier group of shareholders

- **Where**? at the annual meeting in Toronto

- **When**? today

- **Why**? after the computer giant last week posted surprisingly strong earnings for the last quarter

Of course, the full article expands on the *W5* and quotes various sources; however, once you have the *W5*, you have the foundation of the story.

Let's look at some other W leads.

Sample W4 News Lead

You don't always have to use every W in your lead. However, you should be conscious of why you use the ones you use and why you leave out any of them.

Headline: Home prices to tumble in '09

Sub-head: Average decline to be nine percent

Lead: House prices are expected to fall eight percent across Canada this year and sales are predicted to slip nearly 17 percent, according to a new report from The Canadian Real Estate Association.

Deconstructing the W4, we see:

- **Who**: Canadian Real Estate Association

- **What**: house prices expected to fall eight percent

- **Where**: across Canada

- **When**: this year

- **Why**: there was no reference to the economic downturn; however, with the spate of articles on the recession, including others on the same page, the why was left out of the lead. It was, however, briefly addressed later in the article as the cause of the lead.

Shirttail Lead

The Shirttail lead includes a summary lead focusing on the most newsworthy elements. The lead is then followed by a number of related elements.

Lead: The federal government has provided nearly $400 million for desperately needed affordable housing in Ontario—but the money may not be spent any time soon.

The province has stashed the money in a contingency fund pending the outcome of a fiscal battle with Ottawa.

Now, housing groups are wondering whether the province will ever spend the money on housing.

Notice the multiple *who's* and related *what's* in the above lead. Each source has equal weight. Each who is given its own paragraph and its own what to make it clear there are three sides to the story; the conflict makes this topic newsworthy.

Deconstructing the who and what from the above lead we find:

- **Who**: federal government
- **What**: provided nearly $400 million for desperately needed affordable housing
- **Who**: The province
- **What**: has stashed the money in a contingency fund
- **Who**: housing groups
- **What**: are wondering whether the province will ever spend the money on housing

When writing leads, avoid clichés, generalizations, stereotypes, information overload, or any combination of the above, such as:

It's every parent's worst nightmare. Your child is playing outside and you hear the screech of brakes in front of your house followed by a thump.

Many stories start with "It's every parent's worst nightmare" and many of them focus on a silly or mundane topic. If it is truly a nightmare topic, don't tell me. Show me. Let your writing paint a nightmare picture. And if it not a nightmare situation, don't go there.

'Tis the season to be jolly. Ask the man with the white beard, red hat, and that special sparkle in his eye.

While there is technically nothing wrong with the above lead, it is overused during the Christmas season because it is easy to write. I suggest you put more effort into your writing, especially your lead, instead of leaning on something that has been used ad nauseam.

Avoid confusing and overly complex leads too, as the one below:

Nine out of ten doctors in Canada feel socialized medicine is on the road to ruin, but nine out of ten Canadians, while expressing some doubts about the effectiveness of the system, prefer it to the free enterprise American model that leaves many people without adequate medical protection, which is why most Americans, especially those in middle class and lower income brackets, are interested in the Canadian health care system, even though the majority are leery of socialized medicine.

What do the doctors feel? Is it in sync with what Canadians feel? And what are Americans interested in? Furthermore, what do you think this article is really about? You should be enlightened by the lead, not confused by it.

In summary, your lead should focus on the subject matter and convey that focus in a clear, focused and original manner. Read newspaper, magazine and blog article leads on various topics. Try to model the leads you like in your writing.

Not writing news

You might tell me that you won't be writing news so you won't have any need to use the W5. As we saw, the W5 helps us write more effective, focused email. But let's say for a moment you are writing promotional web or blog copy.

After doing right-brain creative work (freefall and clustering) to generate promotional ideas, you can get focused by going linear. To help you move from right-brain to left-brain thinking when faced with a promotional writing project, ask yourself the W5 questions—Who, What, Where, When, Why (and sometimes How)—before you start to write. Get the answers down on paper (or your computer monitor). As you will see, you can answer multiple W questions for many of the W5s.

If you have to do some promotional writing, answer the questions below, or at least the appropriate ones, before you start to write your copy:

- Who is advertising or promoting?

- Who is your target audience?

- Who is the end user—consumer or business?

- What are you advertising or promoting?

- What are the features and benefits associated with the product or service (or event or charity)?

- What need and/or desire does the product fulfill?

- What need and/or desire should you associate with the product?

- Why does the target market need/want/desire the product?

- How does the product or service fulfill the need/want/desire?

- What makes this product different from its competition?

- How does the target market acquire the product or service?

- What action, if any, do you want the target market to take upon reading your copy?

- What incentive (if any) are you offering to induce action?

- When does the incentive to action expire?

- Where is the product or service available?

- When is the product or service available?

- What guarantee is there that the product will live up to expectations generated by the promotional copy?

- "What's in it for me?" (That's your target market asking.)

Most promotional copy will answer some or all of these questions. It depends on the purpose of the ad, the product or service, the target audience. You may not need to use answers to all of those questions in your document. As the writer, though, you should know the answers to the questions before you begin to write so that you can consciously decide what to put in and what to leave out of your copy.

Again, your writing has to capture Attention, hold Interest, influence Attitude and perhaps call for Action. In fact, your writing may have to motivate action. *Try doing all that in a creative vacuum.* Not easy. Try doing it without answers to key questions. Not at all easy. *And try doing it without a process*—a formal approach to writing. Extremely difficult.

Your job then is to be both creative and linear. Then you write with target market and purpose in mind.

Soft Leads

I have had people tell me that they find W5 leads rather pedestrian. To that I say this: if you want online readers to read, then you have to be clear and focused—and sometimes that is pedestrian. At the same time, if you are writing more creative blog posts—human interest articles, for interest—you might want your writing to have more flair. But most of the content on the web is meant to be quickly absorbed and understood and then acted upon. Most of the information on the web is not meant to be a long, leisurely read. It all goes back to your purpose and your audience.

If your purpose is to entertain or inform in a more creative manner, then you may not want to use the W5 lead. I have no problem with that. But if your purpose is to engage your reader as quickly as possible, then you want to use the W5 in your lead.

Soft leads typically burry the news or are used to draw the reader into a longer, more leisurely (sometimes contentious) look at a subject, person, event or situation. The soft leads of feature articles tend to go into more detail to establish the major theme(s) and conflict(s) of the story. Often setting up opposing points of view, the feature lead might focus on a person, recreation of an event or description of a scene or setting.

Again, I have no problem with that—if it suits your purpose and audience. If it does not, and you use the feature lead anyway, you are simply inviting the reader to surf to another page.

With that in mind, allow me to demonstrate a couple of soft leads that deliberately burry the news (many more examples of sort or feature leads, if you are interested, can be found in *Fundamentals of Writing: How to Write Articles, Media Releases, Case Studies, Blog Posts and Social Media Content:* www.paullima.com/books.

> The campaign ad opens with a familiar boyish face, now atop a body that sways uncontrollably. Michael J. Fox, wearing a shirt and suit jacket, talks directly to the camera.
>
> "They say all politics is local, but it's not always the case," Fox says in the 30-second commercial backing Senate candidate Claire McCaskill in Missouri, a Democrat. "What you do in Missouri matters to millions of Americans—Americans like me."
>
> Fox, who suffers from Parkinson's disease and supports research on embryonic stem cell for a potential cure, also has lent his celebrity to Democrats Benjamin L. Cardin, running for the Senate in Maryland, and Wisconsin Gov. Jim Doyle, who is seeking re-election. Both politicians also back stem cell research.

The news is in the paragraph that follows the three paragraph soft lead. The news is not about Fox being diagnosed with Parkinson's disease. That happened well before this article was written and has been fully covered. This article is about Fox and the backlash to his commercials.

Here is the news:

> The ads, released today, have triggered a backlash, with some criticizing them as exploitive. Conservative radio commentator Rush Limbaugh has claimed Fox was "either off his medication or acting."

So the news is about the backlash and the article starts with a soft lead meant to draw the reader in. That, however, does not work well on the web when people what the most pertinent information, and want it sooner rather than later. For instance, I would never use the information below as the lead on my website home page, or even on the about me page, even though it's true:

> Paul Lima considers himself successfully retired from reality. He took a one-year sabbatical from Georgian College in Barrie, Ontario, where he worked as a continuing education program manager, and never returned. Instead, he moved to Toronto and launched a freelance writing business.
>
> That was over 25 years ago.
>
> "I could not see myself going back to work, not to a real job, after a year of freedom," said Lima who writes about technology and business issues for a number of publications and many corporate clients and conducts business-writing training seminars for clients.

Even if I hot-linked "writes about" and "business-writing training," I could not imagine getting many clicks to my writing and training services. The lead is simply not appropriate for my business purposes and my target audience.

You will see in the writing for the web chapter how I actually structure the home page of my website. To repeat, though: Although the above story may be of interest to some readers, it's not how to write copy for my website, given my purpose and target audience. I want to start with the news or most pertinent information about me.

Chapter 9: Put Purpose First

I hope you can see how what we are discussing will make you a stronger writer. Much of it applies to both print and online writing. We will, however, look at specific online writing techniques shortly. With that in mind, I want to look at one more overview topic before we look at online copy and content. At the same time, if you sometimes feel you struggle with sentences and paragraphing, there are chapters on both those topics towards the end of the book.

When it comes to communicating with readers, you want to work your purpose (usually the why of your W5) into the opening of most documents. Doing so ensures that the reader reads all that follows with your purpose in mind. Even if you are simply writing a 140-character tweet, the reader will still want to know why (purpose) you are writing. It may be that you want them to take a particular action (such as click) so your action becomes your purpose.

On occasion, people tell me that starting with purpose feels impolite. My reply? Starting with purpose is effective. For instance, the message below may seem polite but is it effective?

How are you? Hope all is well and that you are not too busy. Hey, maybe we can do lunch next week? By the way, I need your feedback on the environmental report ASAP so I can submit it.

If you start with your purpose, you are more inclined to write:

We need to submit the attached environmental report to the ministry by the end of the month so we can obtain funding. Your feedback is required before the report can be submitted. Please provide feedback by April 21.

As the reader of the second message, I know why you are writing (to get my feedback on the attached report), what I have to do, why I have to do it (to obtain funding) and when I have to do it by. How effective is that? Starting with a sense of purpose translates into almost anything you write for online media. You may not explicitly state your purpose, as you would with an email message, but the reader should know why you are writing and what you want him or her to do or what's in it for the reader if he or she takes your suggested action.

In other words, when you are writing formal documents, you are not writing mystery novels. The reader should not have to unravel your purpose. Instead, you should lead with your purpose or make your purpose clear. Let's use a couple of business examples.

Say you want to inquire about leasing cars for your company from an automotive company. Presumably, your ultimate purpose would be to receive a quote from the company. Based on your purpose, organize the following sentences so that you are starting with purpose. When you are done, you should have an outline for an opening paragraph:

1. General Engines has an excellent reputation for reliable service.

2. We're looking for the best lease price, coupled with reliable service.

3. We would like to receive a quote on the lease of four XK4s.

4. Call us by October 30 to discuss our needs, before issuing the quote.

5. We would like to do business with the local dealer.

Place the points in order, starting with your purpose, before you read on.

Imagine if you had the above five points in front of you before you started to write. What you would do next is

- decide which of the points you should address

- decide which, if any, you should not address

- organize the points you want to address in terms of where you should start, what you should write next and so on

At that point, it's all over but the writing. Write from point to point and you are done. That is the power of organization, no matter what type of document you are writing. Being able to jot down the points you need to address (creating your outline) comes from research or knowing what you need to say to accomplish your purpose.

With that in mind, here is my suggested order, starting with purpose:

1. We would like to receive a quote on the lease of four XK4s.

2. We're looking for the best lease price, coupled with reliable service.

3. General Engines has an excellent reputation for reliable service.

4. We would like to do business with the local dealer.

5. Call us by October 30 to discuss our needs, before issuing a quote.

If I am the leasing manager and I receive this inquiry, I will start thinking about how I can help you—how I can meet your purpose—based on the first point. But what if the leasing manager has moved to the parts department and you don't know it? If I am the former leasing manager, I will open your email message and, based on your first point, I will redirect it to the appropriate person at the dealership. Again, by starting with purpose, you help the reader help you. Not only is your purpose more likely to be met, you are saving the reader time. He does not have to spend time wondering what your email is about. And once you have your points in order, you write. So you might convert your points to a letter like this:

Dear Mr. Lease Manager:

ABC Inc. is looking to receive a quote on the lease of four XK4s. We are interested in the best lease price, coupled with reliable service, <u>for which General Engines has an excellent reputation</u>.

We would like to receive a quote from your local dealer. Please call us by October 30 to discuss our needs in detail, before issuing the quote.

I am not saying the above paragraph represents your entire email. Depending on your relationship with the company, you might want to give the dealership some background information about your organization. If you are putting out a formal tender, you might want to direct the reader to an attachment or an enclosed document. What I am saying is that if you put your purpose first, there are times when you might not have to say much of anything else. And if you do have to write more, at least your reader is reading with *your purpose* in mind.

Notice that I have underlined this phrase: "for which General Engines has an excellent reputation" in the letter. I call such phrases window dressing. They may be nice to write but they do not advance your cause. So why use them? There is no reason to do so. If you cut the phrase, would it be missed? In fact, I suggest that you look for and cut such phrases when you are creating your formal outline so that you don't even write them initially.

Am I adamantly opposed to window dressing? Let me answer the question with a question: How does it help you? If you have one window-dressing phrase, it most likely will not interfere with your communication. If you have one or two window-dressing phrases every paragraph or two, however, your document will not be as clear, concise or coherent as it could be, and should be. That will interfere with the effectiveness of your communication.

Purpose exercise

Let's do another purpose exercise. Review the sentences below. Your purpose is to have the recipient of your message send you a copy of a presentation delivered at the NACB convention. Pick the sentence that *best states your purpose*. You don't have to put all the sentences in order; just pick the one that best states your purpose.

1. I heard good things about the speech you presented on March 15 at the NACB convention.

2. Several managers in my firm have asked me to write you regarding your speech at NACB.

3. Our consulting firm would like to obtain a copy of the speech you gave at the NACB convention last week so we can circulate it internally.

4. As you may know, our company deals with some of the issues you raised recently in your speech at the NACB convention.

5. Do you lend or sell your speeches?

Pick the sentence that best states your purpose, before reading on.

When I conduct workshops based on this book, 95% of the participants pick the third sentence as the one that best states purpose, and I agree with them. Many participants also say that they would not start their letter with that statement, and I don't have a problem with that.

As I have been saying, you should start with purpose. I want to make it clear, however, that you do not have to state your purpose in your opening sentence. You need to define your purpose clearly so you can convey it clearly. But you also have to determine if your purpose sentence will be your opening sentence, middle sentence or the final sentence of your opening paragraph. In other words, you have some latitude—as long as you work your purpose (consider it your topic sentence) into your opening paragraph.

With that in mind, your opening paragraph could read something like this:

I heard good things from my staff about the speech you presented on March 15 at the NACB convention. As you may know, our company deals with some of the issues you raised in your speech. We would like to obtain a copy of the speech you gave at the conference so we can circulate it internally. We are willing to discuss any fee that may be associated with this.

Notice that our purpose is the second last sentence. The reader does not personally know the writer, so there is nothing wrong with providing a bit of back-ground information before hitting the purpose statement.

The point is this: Do you see how much you can pack into a paragraph when you think about what you want to say and write in a clear, concise and coherent manner? Such writing stems from knowing your purpose and organizing your thoughts (creating an outline) before you write. This is what you want to do when writing for any media, including online media.

Practice putting purpose first

Read the following short case studies. When you finish reading each case, jot down your purpose and the action you would like the reader to take. Ask yourself: What is my true business purpose? What do I want to achieve? Why? What action would I like to see the reader take?

Case Study One: Hotel

On business trips to London, Ontario, you stay at the Chelsea Hotel. On your most recent trip, conditions were below expected standards. The room was not clean and dining room service was poor. In addition, the rates had been increased 5%. You travel to London every quarter on business. Your company has used this hotel for several years because it is conveniently located and, even with the recent price increase, offers reasonable rates.

◼ ◼ ◼

Case Study Two: Furniture

On November 1, you ordered furniture from the Office Company catalogue. Your order arrived on November 7 but two chairs were missing. You called and spoke to Harry who said he would take care of it. On November 11, one chair arrived; it was the wrong color. You called and found out that Harry had quit. Nobody else knew about your problem. The person you talked to asked you to email the manager.

Once you have written down your purpose, and the actions you would like to see each reader take, compose opening paragraphs for each of the case studies. (You can review sample openings for each case study in Appendix Two.)

Determine your business purpose for each case study and write an opening paragraph that includes purpose, before you read the paragraphs in Appendix Two.

Chapter 10: Writing for the Web

With the above chapters in mind, let's look at writing for online media—starting with writing for the web.

When it comes to surfing the web, scanning is the new reading. Most web surfers scan web pages; few read web pages word for word.

Most people read more slowly on monitors, even high-resolution ones, than they do on the printed page. They scan to compensate for the extra time it takes to read. You want the copy on your website to capture attention, hold interest, influence attitude and motivate action but you also have to make web pages easy to scan or people will simply leave your website.

There are a number of ways to make web pages easy to scan, as we shall see. However, let's first look at some copy and review its readability (or scannability) quotient.

When I wrote material for the home page of my website, I could have written promotional copy using full sentences and a full paragraph, like this:

Based in Toronto, Paul Lima is a veteran and well-respected freelance writer and business-writing trainer. He has been a freelance writer, copywriter and business-writing instructor for over 25 years. He offers large enterprises, small businesses and organizations a variety of effective business writing and copywriting services and powerful business-writing training seminars. His quality business writing includes case studies, copywriting (brochures, sales letter and other promotional material), web content, media releases, proposals and reports. His proven business-training seminars include business writing and media interview preparation. In addition, he has written several powerful, practical books on topics such as business writing, media release writing and copywriting. Finally, for freelance writers, Paul offers cost-effective and stimulating seminars, e-courses, books and e-books and absolutely free blog content.

Now let's look at the same passage written in what one might describe as a more objective manner—in other words, with the more promotional elements removed.

Based in Toronto, Paul Lima has been a freelance writer, copywriter and business-writing instructor for over 25 years. He offers business writing services and business-writing training seminars. His business writing includes case studies, copywriting, web content, media releases, proposals and reports. His training seminars include business writing and media interview preparation. In addition, he has written several books on business writing, media release writing and copywriting. Finally, Paul offers freelance writers seminars, e-courses, books and blog posts on the business of freelance writing.

Web-based tests show that more objective passages are easier to absorb than more promotional passages because people read web copy differently than they read paper-based documents. That does not make the above passage ideally suited for the web. And if website visitors abandon your copy, no matter how well it is written, it is ineffective writing.

Readability tests, like one conducted by Jakob Nielsen (*How Users Read on the Web*, Jakob Nielsen's Alertbox), analyze web passages based on the following factors:

- **Task time**: Time it takes visitors to find answers to questions pertaining to the text.

- **Memory**: What visitors retain after reading.

- **Errors**: Number of incorrect answers users give for questions that have known answers.

- **Time to recall site structure**: Number of seconds it takes users to recreate a relevant sitemap or navigational menu.

- **Subjective satisfaction**: Ease of finding information, enjoyment of experience, how fresh or tired visitors feel after reading information and completing tasks.

To pass Nielsen's readability test, you want to write concise, focused, non-promotional copy. You also want to make it as easy as possible to scan, using various writing techniques described in this chapter.

The passage below uses bullet points to make the text easy to scan. It also uses hot links that readers can click on if they want more information. In addition, it focuses on the content that a majority of the visitors to the site would want to read. In this way, it cuts down the overall copy volume and it lets those who want more information on a particular topic click on a relevant link.

Based in Toronto, Paul Lima has been a freelance writer and business-writing instructor for over 25 years. He offers companies and organizations a variety of business writing services and business-writing training seminars.

- Business writing: case studies, copywriting (brochures, sales letter and other promotional material), web content, media releases

- Business-writing training: email, letters, proposals, reports, copywriting, web writing, writing media releases

- Books: business writing, media release writing, copywriting, writing articles, blog posts and social media content

But is it too concise?

If you don't want to use bullet points, you can still write easily scannable text. Simply use fewer words and simpler sentences:

Based in Toronto, Paul has been a writer and writing instructor for over 25 years. He offers writing and business-writing training services. He has written several books on writing.

Even though the above passage eschews promotional writing and is easy to scan, one might argue that the passage is too concise—that it leaves out important details—and a reader would not react to it in the appropriate manner. It is your job to recognize that the more copy you include, and the less scannable you make it, the lower the readability or comprehension level will be. However, you also have to keep in mind your purpose, your reader and (sometimes) the wishes of a manager or client. In others words, you might have to walk a fine line between content and scannability. But keep in mind, if the copy is too difficult to scan, it will not be read; you will not accomplish your purpose. The same thing applies if it is too concise.

Hot-link advantage

One thing you can do to reduce copy volume is to use hyperlinks or hot links, as I do in my website copy. In other words, instead of explaining a concept within a paragraph, you link to the concept explanation so readers who want more detail can click and be taken to a page where they can read more or they can click on a link that causes a text box with information to pop up. This reduces word volume you use on the original page, making the copy easier to scan.

In short, hot links let you give people content options while more effectively managing copy volume. You can use hot links to do the following:

- shorten paragraphs and pages to improve readability

- increase page download speeds

- link to background information

- link readers to external sites to demonstrate objectivity

- connect visitors to other web pages, detailed studies (such as PDF files) or even multimedia presentations

When creating hypertext (links) and even page titles (headlines or subheads) keep this in mind: hypertext links and titles act as sign posts and should give people a strong indication of what they will be reading before they click on the link or start to read the copy under the title. People avoid clicking on or reading vague or unknown items.

Now you could argue that about ten words into my website, a reader might click on "freelance writer" and miss the rest of my home page copy. To that I would have to answer, "So?" In other words, I don't mind it if a reader does not read all of my words, as long as the reader gets where the reader wants to go. If the reader is looking for a writer, with one click and the reader is on my writing page. Not every website will want to get the reader clicking so soon. But that should be a conscious decision that you make: when you want the reader to click and what you want the reader to click on.

In short, I'd like to think that my website copy engages visitors and that it speaks to readers and not at them. To do so, you include words people can relate to, and you avoid jargon, business speak and buzz words. In other words, you write using plain English (or whatever language your website is in).

But what about purpose? Have I put that upfront? Remember, you cannot do so unless you define your purpose. You might say that my purpose is to sell my writing and training services, and it is. However, what is the reader's purpose? Look at my page headline at www.paullima.com and you will see this phrase: "the right words. on time. on budget." I believe that most people who come to my website are looking for the right words—either to have me write them or to train them to produce them. And they are looking to get the writing or training on time and on budget. So my slogan, as it were, placed strategically on the top of my page, addresses the reader's purpose for coming to my website and tells the reader why they should pick me— which is my purpose after all.

When we get to landing pages (the pages that readers land on when they click on online ads), you will see that I advocate giving readers something more to click on upfront while still giving readers who need more information something to click on after they have read more about your product or service. But let's look at hot links on websites a bit more.

The following passage from the Canadian Cancer Society website (March, 2006) uses a subhead to capture the attention of readers who are interested in 2006 cancer research grants awarded in Ontario (their purpose for coming to the site) and links people to grants by city and type and to a complete list of the grants. In other words, the website's purpose is to convey information that fulfills the purpose of site visitors. In other words, put purpose first. Here is the copy:

2006 Research Grants in Ontario

Cancer researchers in Ontario received $18.7 million from the Canadian Cancer Society in 2006. Thirty-eight new grants were awarded to researchers in <u>Hamilton</u>, <u>Kingston</u>, <u>London</u>, <u>Ottawa</u> and <u>Toronto</u> for promising research in several areas, including <u>skin cancer prevention</u> and <u>using viruses to stimulate a person's immune system</u> to fight cancer. Of the 72 new grants awarded across the country, 38 are going to Ontario researchers.

View complete list of Canadian Cancer Society-funded research projects in Ontario.

If you are interested in grants received by cancer researchers in various cities, you have clickable options. If you are interested in grants received by topic or type of cancer, you have options. And if you want to see all the grants, you have an option.

Hot links can also be used to present different content at different levels to different audiences. For instance, not every person who reads the copy on testicular self-examination will want to perform a self-exam, but they at least want to more about the disease (the reader's purpose), otherwise they would not be on the site. The hot-linked text takes those readers who want to conduct a self-examination to a page where they can find out how to do so. Notice, also, how other words and phrases in the passage are linked to additional information for those who want to know more about various aspects of this disease.

Performing testicular self-examination (TSE) regularly helps you learn what is normal for your testicles so that you will be able to notice changes. See your doctor if you notice anything unusual.

Click here to learn how to perform a self-examination.

In short, if you don't know your purpose and the reader's purpose, how can you write to achieve either?

Format fonts and subheads

To draw a reader's eye through a passage, you can use **bold type**, *italicized type*, underlined type or color variations. However, I caution against excess use of these techniques, as well as against use of multiple typefaces (also known as typestyles or fonts) and type sizes, because a variety of formats, fonts and sizes can be distracting and even misleading. For instance, website readers often expect text that is formatted differently to be hot linked. They might click on your formatted text expecting to be taken to another page. However, if you use such variations judiciously, such as bold subheads or bold words or phrases at the beginning of sentences, they can be an effective way to help your readers scan.

Another effective way to use text variations to help readers scan is to use *meaningful* subheads as well as bold ones. Notice the emphasis on meaningful. Web readers want meaningful, not clever, information. When it comes to the use of headlines and subheads, they want copy that says, "Hey, this is about x, which is something you are interested in; otherwise, you would not have used x in your Google search."

If you review the pages of this book, you will see that I frequently use meaningful subheads. Occasionally, I use clever ones (or ones that I think are clever). I could use subheads more frequently and I could eliminate my attempts at being clever. However, you are a captive audience, one that has purchased this book and has a sense of purpose that this book is supposed to help you fulfill. That does not mean I should make this book difficult to read, nor does it mean that I can get away with taking too many liberties. At the same time, I don't have to write as if I were writing web content. However, I'd like to think that my writing here, as well as online, engages you, the reader. I'd like to think that it speaks to you, and not at you, because it includes words and concepts you can relate to and it avoids jargon, business speak, and buzz words. In other words, I am attempting to write using plain English not a convoluted or complex English. In short, I don't use *humungous* words when *big* ones will do, so to speak.

So think about your subheads, or minor topic points on a page that addresses a major topic (which you should have outlined) as you write. And use clear bold subheads to help your reader through the page.

Other techniques to assist scanning

Inverted pyramid. The inverted pyramid packs the most pertinent who, what, where, when, why and how information into the opening paragraph or two of an article, as in the examples we have seen and in this example from the *New York Times* (April 13, 2010):

> Two Democratic state lawmakers have sponsored a bill that would give principals in New York City the power to choose who should lose their jobs if the city needs to lay off teachers because of budget cuts, contradicting the current law under which teachers who have

been in the system for the shortest amount of time would be the first
to lose their jobs.

Take a moment and review the W5:

- *Who?* Two Democratic state lawmakers

- *What?* Have sponsored a bill that would give principals in New York
  City the power to choose who should lose their jobs

- *Where?* New York

- *When?* Yesterday is implied; this news article was published the day
  after the bill was sponsored

- *Why?* If the city needs to lay off teachers because of budget cuts

Since most website visitors read the first paragraph or two before deciding if
they will read on or not (some studies indicate *read/don't read* decisions are made even
more quickly), packing the W5 into the opening paragraph ensures the reader sees the
most important information you want to convey.

One idea per paragraph. To make it easier for readers to scan, try to use no
more than one idea per paragraph. This will help you keep your paragraphs short,
which will create more white space and make the document look easier to read. That
psychology (that the page is easy to read) is important.

Bulleted or numbered lists. As discussed, bulleted (or numbered) points are
easier to scan than full block paragraphs. (See Chapter 20, Constructing Paragraphs,
for more information on when to use bullet points as opposed to numbered points.)

Use fewer words. If you take the W5 approach, you can say a lot in very few
words. Even if you have a lot to say, ask yourself if some readers only need a synopsis
or summary—like an executive summary in a formal report. Combine the synopsis or
summary with the power of the hot link to offer readers who want more information
the opportunity to click to read more.

Web writing in action

An April 27, 2009, online article written by Jakob Nielsen demonstrates how
BBC News effectively harnesses the power of writing for the web. Nelson conveys
this information by harnessing the power of writing for the web too.

The article starts with a summary. Even though web writing should be concise and brief, Nielsen presents an even more concise summary to help readers decide, based on their objectives, if the article is worth reading. In addition, he uses hyperlinks to keep the article short and bullet points and the judicious use of bold points to make his article easier to scan, absorb and understand. If the reader is particularly interested in a section that contains a hyperlink, the reader can click. Otherwise, the reader can read on.

Notice in particular how he bolds the first part of the bullet point. Why does he do this? Studies show many readers do not even read to the end of a line when scanning web copy. Using bold judiciously pulls the reader's eye to the point because the eye sees the bold and the brain thinks: This could be important; I'd better go there.

Having said that about how Nielsen writes effectively for the web, I want to restate that the article is about how the BBC News effectively harnesses the power of writing for the web.

World's Best Headlines: BBC News

Summary: Precise communication in a handful of words? The editors at BBC News achieve it every day, offering remarkable headline usability.

It's hard enough to <u>write for the web</u> and meet the guidelines for <u>concise, scannable and objective content</u>. It's even harder to write web headlines, which must be:

- **short** (because people don't read much online);

- **rich in information scent**, clearly summarizing the target article;

- **front-loaded** with the most important keywords (because users often <u>scan the beginning</u> of list items);

- **understandable out of context** (because headlines often appear without articles, as in search engine results); and

- **predictable**, so users know whether they'll like the full article before they click (because people don't return to sites that promise more than they deliver).

For several years, I've been impressed with BBC News headlines, both on the main BBC home page and on its dedicated news page. Most sites routinely violate headline guidelines but BBC editors consistently do an awesome job.

Concise and Informative

On a recent visit, the BBC list of headlines for "other top stories" read as follows:

- Italy buries first quake victims

- Romania blamed over Moldova riots

- Ten arrested in UK anti-terrorism raids

- Villagers hurt in West Bank clash

- Mass Thai protest over leadership

- Iran accuses journalist of spying

- Around the world in 38 words

The average headline consumed a mere 5 words and 34 characters. The amount of meaning they squeezed into this brief space is incredible: every word works hard for its living.

Each headline conveys the gist of the story on its own, without requiring you to click. Even better, each gives you a good idea of what you'll get if you do click and lets you judge—with a high degree of confidence—whether you'll be interested in the full article. As a result, you won't waste clicks. You'll click through to exactly those news items you want to read.

– Jakob Nielsen's Alertbox, April 27, 2009 (www.useit.com/alertbox)

Again, notice how the bold subheads and the bold words starting the various points act as signposts and give people a strong indication of what is there even before their eyes leave the words. People avoid reading unknown items or, even worse, ignore them all together. And in each BBC headline ask who, what, where, when and why, and you will find the most pertinent Ws addressed. That is concise, effective communication that lets the right reader click on the right article for the right reasons.

Why concise web writing?

You should have a solid understanding of the need for concise, easy-to-read web writing. If you need this concept reinforced, think of website visitors as being engaged in hit-and-run information retrieval. They look at websites in this manner:

- Is the site interesting? If so, click, retrieve, move on

- If not, move on

It is your job to accommodate hit-and-run visitors. To do so, you have to use the techniques outlined above. However, you will also want to do the following:

- use plain language that readers understand

- present chunks or screen-sized passages of text that convey your purpose and help your audience do what they want to do (or you want them to do) on your site

-

Chapter 11: Web Writing in Action

Although the home page of my website (www.paullima.com) is not perfect, I'd like to think it embodies most of the writing-for-the-web principles espoused here.

The page includes my image, which may be its major flaw, and my slogan, which I hope captures the attention of the site visitor by appealing to their sense of purpose. Below my slogan is the primary menu, taking visitors to my most important pages. What then follows is a brief description about my services. Again, notice the hot links in the description, making it easy for visitors who know what they want to quickly click on the appropriate page.

freelance writer/writing trainer
media relations/interview consultant
freelance writer/writing trainer
media relations/interview consultant

paul lima: the right words. on time. on budget.

Home | About | Contact | Writing | Training | Books

Business Writer and Business-Writing Trainer

Case studies. Website, blog and social media content. Media releases. Promotional copy. Do you require clear, concise, *focused* writing to promote your business, product, service or event? With 25+ years of business writing and promotional writing experience, Toronto **freelance writer** and **copywriter** Paul Lima delivers *the right words, on time and on budget.*

Business writing - email, letters, proposals, reports. Writing for the web. Copywriting. Writing media releases. Do you want your staff to write clear, concise, focused messages, documents and other content? As a qualified **business-writing trainer**, Paul can train your staff to write effectively and efficiently.

Paul's freelance writing and business training services include:

- **Freelance Writing** - case studies, media releases, copywriting, SEO copywriting, web content, blog posts, reports and proposals
- **Business Training** - business and email writing, copywriting, writing for the web, writing media releases and media interview training

If you want an **effective business writer** working for you, or an **experienced trainer** conducting business-writing seminars for your staff, **contact Paul today**.

Paul has worked for companies in a variety of sectors, including IT, e-commerce, telecom, broadcast, banking and financial services, education, retail, food and beverage, transportation, social services and health and safety. He has also written **several books** on business writing, copywriting, media release writing and preparing for media interviews.

Contact | Business Writing | Business Training | Media Interview Training | Books on Writing
For Freelance Writers | e-Courses | News Articles | Creative Writing | Site Map | **Blog**

In short, when you visit my home page (as illustrated above), you see concise, focused copy that is easy to scan. In addition, you are given multiple ways of getting to the most important inside pages.

Writing long for the web

If you have a media release, a report or any other long document that you want to share with website visitors, you do not have to rewrite it for the web. In other words, you can post print-based documents and material on a website as Adobe Acrobat PDF files or even as long website pages. However, you don't want to use such documents as your home page or a product or service feature page.

What you can do is link to print-based documents (such as PDFs) from an appropriate website page. Consider writing a summary or abstract of the document (kind of like an executive summary) so the readers have details about what they are clicking through to. And, since this is the web, expect some readers to read the summary and move on. If the summary is well written, readers might get all they need. However, if the document is critical and you really want it read, consider creating a web-friendly version of it to help your website visitors read it.

Use a consistent navigational structure

If you look at the navigation structure or page menu on paullima.com, you will see it is used consistently on every page. The reason is simple: from any page, I would like my visitors to be able to get to any page on the website. Website visitors would like this too. They don't like having to constantly hit the back button to get to a page where they've been or hit "home" to start looking all over again for a page they want to get to.

Here is my structure:

Home | About | Contact | Writing | Training | Books

When you think about it, from any page on my website a visitor can get home, read about me, contact me, read about my writing or training services or read about my books. Your navigational structure should be consistent too.

Am I saying don't ever break the rules?

Not at all. However, if you are going to break the rules, have a solid reason for doing so. In other words, don't break the rules and frustrate your visitors. It's way too easy to leave a website and that's what visitors will do if you frustrate them.

A website like MSN.com breaks the rules, but look at how it breaks them. Here is the main navigation menu on the MSN home page:

Autos | Entertainment | Flyers | News | Lifestyle | Money | Music | Sports | Tech | Travel | Video | Weather | My MSN | More

If you go to the website, you will notice that there is a sub-menu under each main menu item. For instance, if you look under Entertainment you see the following links:

Movies | Music | Celebs | TV | Games | Videos

In other words, the system is set up to make it easy for visitors to quickly get exactly where they want to go. Since it is highly unlikely that someone who goes to Celebs will want to go to, say, Autos, next, the main menu is not repeated on the Celebs page. There is, however, a sub-menu under Celebs. In addition, just in case the visitor wants to go somewhere completely different, there is a home button on every page. And there you have the consistency: anyone can drill down in the category they select or they can go home from any page. This is important because the site is complex. Unlikely that they will want to go home, but it's still easy to do so.

When you are setting up your menu link names, just as when you are writing headlines, titles and subheads, use words that quickly give people a strong indication of what will happen even before they click because people avoid clicking on vague or unknown items.

Chapter 12: Other Web-writing Hints and Tips

Before we move on to writing short ads, landing pages, blog posts and social media content, here are some other hints and tips that you will want to keep in mind when writing web copy. Many of them apply to writing blog content and social media content, so keep them in mind whenever you are writing for any online medium. As always, these rules can be broken. But think about them and before you break them, and break them only if it will support your purpose and enable you to more clearly speak to your target audience.

Front-load content. Front loading means putting the conclusion first, followed by the pertinent who, what, where, when, why and how elements. The first line of each paragraph should contain the conclusion for that paragraph, so site visitors can quickly scan through the opening sentence, instantly understand what the paragraph is about and decide if they want to read the rest of the paragraph or not. See the starting with topic sentences section in Chapter 19 (Writing Sentences).

Left-aligned text. Also known as ragged right, such text is easier to read than justified text, which in turn is easier to read than centre- or right-aligned text. When reading through justified text (as most books use) the spacing between each word is different so our eyes have to search for the next word. On monitors and screens, this slows down our reading speed. Right- and centre-aligned paragraphs slow down reading speed even more because each time you finish reading one line your eye has to search for the beginning of the next line.

Avoid excess punctuation. If a reader sees a sentence with more than one comma, the sentence looks like it is hard to scan and is therefore likely to turn off a reader.

That doesn't mean that you should punctuate improperly online but keep your sentence simple; avoid the use of advanced punctuation marks such as semi-colons and colons: start new sentences instead. (Or we might write this online: Punctuate properly. Keep sentence simple. Avoid semi-colons and colons. Start new sentences instead.)

Here is another example: "It is really important to keep three principles in mind, when thinking of the best shirts to buy: comfort, style, and eco-impact." Instead, you might rewrite for the web like this: "Keep comfort, style and eco-impact in mind when buying shirts."

Use one space after a period. If you took typing in high school (yes, on a typewriter) using two spaces after a period was drilled into your head. The convention for web writing (and for any writing using a word processor) is now one space after a period.

Don't begin sentences with "But," "And," "Or," "Because" or "Yet." Although doing so can be technically correct, there are readers who think it is grammatically incorrect. Exceptions? As any copywriter will tell you, if writing promotional copy you may want to begin a sentence with word like "and" or "because" for effect. But do not to overdo it. Or, as we might write online: Don't overdo it.

Keep sentences short. Enough said.

Use subheads. Subheads make your writing easier to scan. They also let the reader know what is coming up. While all your words are important, online readers often want to get to the information they are looking for so they can absorb it and move on. Make it hard to find, and they will simply move on. Call it the Google effect. If the surfer can't find what he or she is looking for on your page, the surfer will simple search for it again and find it elsewhere.

Capitalize words in headlines and subheads. Doing so makes them easier to scan. Avoid, however, capitalizing prepositions such as of, to, for is, and, but, or or the.

Use spell check *and* your eyes. If you spell "breakfast" as "break fast" the spell check might not pick up on your mistake. Proofread what you have written. If it's critical that it be error free, hirer an editor or proofreader (something I admit I should have done with this book). Simply put, people won't trust your brand or product if your website is full of spelling and grammatical errors.

Spell out phrases before using the acronym. CMA can stand for Certified Management Accountant, Canadian Medical Association, Canadian Marketing Association and Canadian Museum Association. Unless what you are writing about is perfectly clear from the context, and even if it is, the first time you use a phrase spell it out in full and put the acronym in brackets. If you use the phrase again, you can use the acronym. So the first time, you would write: "According to the Canadian Marketing Association (CMA), most Canadians are watching movies online now…"

Minimize use of literary devices. Keep the use of metaphors, similes, or other literary device to a minimum, if you use them at all. Now if you are posting a literary short story that you want readers to luxuriate in, you would write as creatively as possible. However, if you are writing something you want readers to absorb quickly so they will take action, make your points as clearly as possible.

To summarize

When it comes to writing for a website, you need to know and do the following:

- Know your purpose before you begin so you can focus on achieving your purpose

- When appropriate, make sure you clearly state your purpose or imply it—depending on what you are writing about

- Make your writing easy to scan and absorb, in other words, don't write in a overly promotional style

- Write in a concise manner, but don't be too concise; I know, it can be a balancing act, so keep your purpose and readers in mind

- Write in the inverted pyramid style; think W5 when writing; use the important Ws in each paragraph

- Keep paragraphs relatively short; use bullet points or numbered points when and where it makes sense to do so

- Judiciously use bold, italics and colored type; don't over use such features or you will lose focus

- Use bullet points and numbered points where appropriate; start such points with bold words or phrases

- Use subheads to make the page easier to scan

- Use hot links to allow visitors to quickly get where they want to go and to keep your paragraphs shorter

- Use a consistent navigational structure, or at least one that makes sense to your website and your visitors

Chapter 13: Direct Response Marketing

Note: This chapter on direct response marketing (DRM) sets the stage for writing short online ads and website landing pages (pages you direct people to through online or offline advertising). You can read more about advertising copywriting in my book, *Copywriting That Works: Bright Ideas to Help You Inform, Persuade, Motivate and Sell!*

The communication process

Before we look at DRM (marketing meant to quickly solicit an immediate action or direct response), online ads and website landing pages, I want to review the communication process introduced in Chapter One.

As we have seen, communication requires a sender who sends a message through a channel to a receiver. However, the process is not complete without feedback, which closes the communication loop. Businesses that advertise want feedback so they can measure the effectiveness of online and off-line DRM promotions. The method used to solicit feedback often changes based on the medium and the purpose of the message.

For instance, an advertiser who wants to solicit feedback based on an online or print ad that is meant to raise brand awareness might survey a segment of the target market before and after the ad runs to determine if the ad has raised awareness. An advertiser interested in sales may look at sales and store and/or website traffic on the day(s) the ad runs and for a few days afterwards. In addition, an online business is able to track traffic or click-throughs generated by various online and email promotions.

In DRM, the advertiser wants to solicit immediate feedback (response) directly from the message receiver or viewer. For instance, if an advertiser sends an electronic newsletter to an email list, the advertising might request that readers click on a link to a website. Count the clicks, and you have feedback on your request. An advertiser who sends a direct mail flyer to a mailing list might ask recipients to call a toll-free number and enter a specific code to receive more information. Count the calls, and you have feedback. In other words, if the purpose of the email ad is to motivate an action such as visiting a website, then click-throughs from the email to the website, which can be automatically measured, constitute feedback. If the purpose is to get the audience to call for more information, then calls for more information constitute feedback.

Gauging versus motivating

When it comes to DRM, motivating action that can be gauged is paramount. However, if you do not motivate action, you will have little feedback to gauge. Which begs the question: how do you motivate action, such as a click, call or an actual sale?

When you motivate sales, you use incentives to motivate people to give you feedback (to take action such as buy something). Before you can motivate action, you have to capture attention, maintain interest and influence attitude, as we have said. However, if you want action, it is your job to define the action you want and then to motivate it—to give your target market an incentive to act. A simple method of motivating action is to include a coupon in an ad—something like a "buy one bag of potato chips get a second bag free" coupon. An online software advertiser might create a banner ad or Google ad that mentions a thirty-day free trial offer.

Online DRM ads tend to focus on motivating readers to click. The click takes readers to a website landing page where they can read information that, in theory, motivates them to take the next step—buy the product, request a callback from a sales representative, donate to a charity, support a cause and so on. The DRM call to action frequently (but not always) also includes incentives to motivate the target market to act.

Hook, line and sinker

To capture attention, hold interest, influence attitude and to motivate readers to act, the DRM ad uses the hook, line and sinker approach to marketing.

Hook. To hook the target market, the advertiser uses various landmark words with which the target market can identify. Often, in business-to-consumer DRM, the writer's job is to capture attention (hook the reader) by creating desire and promising fulfillment. In business-to-business DRM, however, the writer's job is to hook the reader by identifying a problem and offering a solution or identifying an opportunity and offering a way to help the reader take advantage of it.

Line. The body copy, or line, reinforces how the product or service solves the problem, fills the need or satisfies the desire. It builds trust, often by reassuring the client through guarantees and testimonials. It also may anticipate and overcome objections because people will not act if they have objections. In short, the body copy or line presents information that will influence the attitude of the target market. The people in the target market need to have their attitude influenced before they will take action.

Sinker. This is the call to action. It tells readers what the advertiser wants them to do, how to do it, where to do it and when to do it. It generally uses a time-limited offer (incentive)—such as a sale price or some other discount, a special offer, a free trial, a contest and so on—to motivate the reader to buy the product, visit a website, call for a demo, make an appointment with a sales representative, fill out a survey that further qualifies the target market and so forth. In some DRM advertising, the hook actually alludes to the incentive as a kind of teaser that motivates the reader to read. The sinker, however, motivated the reader to act and tells them how to act.

Focus on the prospect, not the product

Before writing business-to-business DRM material, the most useful background research you can do is to ask your typical prospect: "What's the biggest problem or opportunity you have right now?" By ensuring the copy addresses that issue, you focus on the needs of the prospect. Of course, you will tie that answer into the features and benefits of the product or service you are offering—but you will put the prospect first. You will, in short, answer this prospect question: What's in it for me? Prospects have to think there is something in it for them before they will act.

That can also be the case in business-to-consumer DRM. Ideally, your copy focuses on the greatest desire or aspiration of the target market. However, you can still think of it in terms of problem/solution. If the target market cannot achieve his or her desires and aspirations, the target market has a problem. And that, for the advertiser, is an opportunity to offer a solution.

DRM writing process

There are several steps you should take before writing a DRM brochure or website landing page, such as defining or determining the following:

- sales/marketing objective or purpose
- target market demographics
- target market's issue, problem, opportunity, need or desire
- target market's objections
- specific objection you must overcome
- how to overcome them
- how to build trust

- your call to action

- incentive to motivate action

Again, if you are creating an online ad meant to motivate a click (response), you will not address all those points, as we will see when we examine Google ads. However, you still have to capture attention and motivate action—the click. No small order that. Once readers click, they land on the landing page—the page that covers all the points outlined above to help the reader make a buy decision.

What About Direct Response Email Marketing?

Direct response email marketing is less costly than printed DRM material that is mailed to the target market. Email campaigns cost $5 to $7 per thousand, compared with the $500 to $750 (or more) per thousand for direct mail. As well, they are quicker to execute, they get faster results and their success (or failure) can be measured more easily (by click-throughs and sales the day the email lands).

Email marketing is not spam, if used on an opt-in or permission basis. However, there are risks to sending DRM email. Email users are so overwhelmed by spam that they use a number of filtering techniques to keep it out of their in-boxes. DRM email may be caught in spam filters. Occasionally, email users forget that they have granted permission for a marketer to send them email and they may view the DRM email as spam.

The challenge for email marketers is to make the message so relevant to the person receiving it that it is not confused with spam. And the offer must be compelling enough to make the recipient act on it.

Email marketers should:

- Use strong, provocative or self-explanatory subjects lines

- Keep the message to one computer screen (page)

- Include a link to a website for more information

- Include an incentive to click on the link

- Include unsubscribe information

- Ensure those who unsubscribe get off the email list

Chapter 14: Writing Short Web Ads

When it comes to writing for the web, writing Google ads is about as short as it gets. If you conduct a search for "Google ads," you'll find scores of search engine links to sites with information on Google ads. It does not cost anything to have a web page indexed in the Google search engine. However, if my website had information about Google ads and it was ranked one million links down, visitors would never find my site. To combat a low rank, I can set up an ad on Google using Google AdWords:

Top Website Advertising
www.INeedHits.com/web-advertising
Get your Website found on 1st page.
Get Your $80 Free Advertising Now!

This particular ad was listed number one (results are subject to change) when I used the search term "Google ads." How did the advertiser manage to get the ad listed first? He used Google AdWords to set up the ad to show up when Google visitors search for keywords related to Google ads and he paid more per click than others who associated similar ads with keywords related to Google ads.

Writing Google ads

When we look more closely at the number one ranked ad based on the search term "Google ads" (at the time of writing this book), we see the following:

1. Hook or attention-grabbing headline: "Top Website Advertising"

2. Line or interest-holding body copy: "Get your Website found on 1st page"

3. Sinker or incentive to motivate the click: "Get Your $80 Free Advertising Now!"

Even though there are only three lines of actual copy, that sounds a lot like writing a DRM ad, does it not?

With AdWords, you create your own ad, choose keywords to help Google match your ad to your audience's search terms and pay only when someone clicks on your ad. The more you are willing to pay and the more times people click on your ad, the higher your ad ranks. Since rank for Google ads is a combination of the price you pay and how popular your ad is, based on clicks, your copy should be effective enough to encourage clicks.

Let me repeat that: *Your copy should be effective enough to encourage clicks.* When you place an ad on Google, you want a response—a click. In short, Google ads are four-line DRM ads.

AdWords character (letters, symbols, spaces) limitations are strict. You cannot go over character count when you create your headline, two lines of text and your display URL or website address. Here are the maximum character counts:

- **Headline**: 25 characters

- **Display URL**: 35 characters

- **Line 1**: 35 characters

- **Line 2**: 35 characters

Note that the above character counts are for ads that appear on the right side of the page in search results, not for the Google ads that appear at the top of the page. You get to link your ad to any keywords you want to. Let's look at a few Google Ads and their keywords. What happens if I search for "coffee delivery?" I see eight ads. Here are three of them:

Coffee Order
www.communitycoffee.com
Official Community Coffee Site,
Shop for coffee online and save!

Coffee Delivery
www.BizRate.com
Find Best Bargain Prices On
Fast Quality Coffee Delivery!

Coffee delivery
www.coffeefarm.com
Enjoy Specialty Coffee Delivered
Right To Your Door. Best Prices.

Now what happens if I search for "coffee delivery Toronto?" I see five ads. Some are the same as the "coffee delivery" ads, but look at this one:

Coffee Services –Toronto
www.mrcase.com
Home & Office Delivery By The Case.
Serving The GTA For Over 20 Years!

Mr. Case only delivers coffee in the greater Toronto area (GTA), so it would make no sense for Mr. Case to compete with the companies that have their ads set to appear when someone types in the keywords "coffee delivery." Instead, Mr. Case's ad is linked to the keywords "coffee delivery Toronto" to reflect the geographical area it services. And the ad copy reinforces that. It says "GTA." If you don't know what the GTA is (i.e. you do not live or work in the GTA), Mr. Case is hoping you will not click on the ad, because the company cannot service your coffee needs.

Let's look more closely at the Mr. Case ad. While not quite a hook, line and sinker, we do see elements of DRM advertising. The headline (Coffee Services – Toronto) speaks directly to the target market—the person who typed the search term "coffee delivery Toronto." So it hooks or captures attention. The second copy line reinforces the delivery concept, and "by the case" gets me thinking about price—they must sell at a discount if they deliver by the case.

The third copy line builds trust by overcoming a possible objection: Who are these people? I've never heard of them. Perhaps I've never heard of them, but they have been "Serving The GTA For Over 20 Years!"

All right, then. I trust them. *Click*! Even though there is no actual sinker.

Now let's go to Google and search for something computer-oriented: contact management software. Let's look at one of the software ads:

Contact Mgt Software
www.NetSuite.com
Fully integrated with Outlook.
30-day free trial.

Isn't that headline boring? All it does is repeat what might be the keywords a person typed in when conducting a search. But wait a minute! What was the searcher looking for? Does that headline not tell searchers that they have found exactly what they were looking for? If the searchers happen to use Outlook, as many businesses do, they are interested. And there's a free trial, what do they have to lose? Click. And the searcher is on the landing page, the page that then tries to sell them or, in this case, motivate them to try the product for free. (We'll look at landing page copy in the next chapter.)

In summary, you can pack a lot into a few short lines—including a hook, line and sinker. In many ways, that's what writing for the web is all about—saying as much as you can in as few words as possible. However, you do not want to use so few words that your readers miss your point and do not know what you want them to do. Keep that in mind as you are writing web-based copy (or pretty much any copy or any messages for that matter).

Note: Google is now running ads above the free listings that show up based on search results. These ads have a different layout than ads that run down the right side of Google search results. However, the same principles apply: you want to use the hook, line and sinker approach to generate a click.

Now What?

See if you can write a couple of Google Ads using the hook, line and sinker format. Speak to your target market using words, phrases and concepts that they can identify with, or that reflect their needs or desires, build trust and motivate the reader to act (click).

Remember that your target market has pre-qualified itself by entering keywords related to your ad—keywords that you chose to associate with your ad. They are hot prospects. Who could ask for anything more?

Now pick your products and create some Google Ads. Don't forget to follow the Google AdSense character count. If you go over the character count, your ad will not run. Within the limitations of that count, capture your reader's attention with a hook, hold the reader's attention with a line and see if you can motivate action with a sinker.

Chapter 15: Website Landing Pages

When it comes to DRM and the web, all the rules apply—more or less. What's cool about the web is that prospects often find you by using search engines. They enter keywords related to what you are offering and up pops a link and/or ad related to your website. The searcher, who has prequalified himself or herself by entering keywords related to your product, service or cause, clicks on the link and lands on your home page or any other page you have optimized to show up in a search engine based on specific search terms.

If the pre-qualified searcher clicks on a Google ad (known as AdWords) the ad should take the prospect to a landing page—your online DRM page—not to your website home page.

What's the difference between a home page and a landing page? A home page has a web address such as www.yoursite.com and generally includes links to all the main pages on a website. A landing page might have a web address such as www.-yoursite.com/product-info and is set up to solicit a direct response from a prospect that lands on it after clicking on an ad or some other link.

In short, a landing page is a web page that users click to from an online ad. Landing pages are used by advertisers who wish to provide a special offer in response to a click-through on a banner ad or search engine pay-per-click (PPC) ad, such as a Google ad. For best results, landing pages should be highly targeted to the person who might click on the ad and are set up using DRM principles.

Although landing pages do not need all the elements print DRM brochures require, they can offer more information than DRM brochures because of "the hot-link advantage." The hot-link advantage lets you incorporate links on your landing page so visitors can click on them for more information. For instance, you can create a link from the landing page to the full list of features and benefits or to the complete details of your guarantee.

Having said that, some advertisers believe you should put everything you want to say about your product or service on one landing page. This makes for longer landing pages and is often used in business-to-consumer sales. Whether you include all the copy required to close the sale on the landing page, or on the landing page and on various hot-linked pages (a debate that can be left for another book), you still need a hook, line and sinker on the landing page. However, the first thing you typically need is a call to action, perhaps in conjunction with a sinker.

Why a call to action first? Think about it. Landing page visitors are hot prospects. They pre-qualified themselves by using keywords related to your product and clicked on a Google ad about your product. Why not offer such visitors a way to buy—a link that says "Buy Now!" or at least "Try Now!" (if you are selling software, for instance)? If the visitors are hot prospects, they can buy right away. If they are just curious, they can continue to read your landing page copy. And yes, there are times you may want to break this "rule" but do it with your purpose and target market in mind.

Busy as a bee

Below is the landing page for U-Rent-It Manager (URIM), a party/event and small equipment rental order-entry and reservation software system. (The application is real; the name has been changed.) If you have ever rented equipment or tools, you probably feel lucky if the reserved equipment is there when you show up. The equipment rental staff is running around like chickens with their heads cut off and you wonder if they actually know what they are doing. The folks are busy, no doubt about it. But are they organized?

The URIM application organizes inventory and staff so that rental customers get the products they have reserved. URIM has a Google AdWords campaign. The ads take prospects to the URIM landing page where the first thing visitors see is a link to a thirty-day free trial offer for the application. Click on the link and you see guarantees and other trust-building copy, as well as a link to the terms and conditions (kept as simple as possible) and, of course, the download link.

The sales offer (even though it is a free trial) is put up front because visitors have prequalified themselves by using keywords to search for such a product and just might want to try it. So why not make it easy to try? (Layout and design are important to make the page easy to read and the requested action easy to follow.)

What if the visitor needs convincing? The page contains sales and promotional copy as well. Notice the use of bullet points in the sample copy below. As discussed, they make copy easy to scan. Often the designer will indicate where bullet points should be placed but the copywriter can also make the suggestion.

Here is URIM's landing page copy (with the initial graphic "try" offer removed):

Busy as a bee? But are you as efficient?

- Get everyone in your hive working together
- Take the guesswork out of inventory tracking and planning
- Eliminate recopying and re-keying orders
- Deliver the right product to the right client, at the right time
- Spend more time growing your business!

The beehive may look like a chaotic site but it is efficiency in motion. U-Rent-It Manager (URIM) is a party/event rental and small equipment rental order-entry and reservation system that can bring beehive efficiency to your business.

With online inventory tracking and sales and order calculations, URIM will have you buzzing with excitement.

Remove the guesswork

URIM takes the guesswork out of inventory tracking and planning and eliminates the need to recopy or re-enter orders. URIM includes contact manager and marketing functions and a "one-button click" to export accounting data to QuickBooks.

URIM is a cost-effective way to combat chaos and introduce order to your rental business. It saves you time and makes your hive a more productive place.

Designed with valuable input from the party/event and small equipment rental industry, and fully supported by phone, email and online support, URIM is an intuitive application that will have you seeing positive results in a few hours.

Right product, right person, right time

Get the right product to the right person at the right time. Generate increased customer satisfaction and repeat business. Create more time to expand your business. Produce more honey. Now that's sweet!

Hive in Action: URIM Features and Benefits

Free Taste of Rental Manager: Download Demo

Build Your Hive: Purchase URIM

Notice the hot links at the end of the landing page copy. If readers want to know more, they can click on features and benefits. If they want to try the product at no charge, they can click on the "try" link. If they want to buy, they can do that too. On the demo page, prospects find guarantees and other trust-building copy. On all the pages, they find links back to the landing page and links to all the other pages.

Here is copy from the Hive in Action: URIM Features and Benefits page:

Transform your business into a hive of productivity

> "When I finally decided to update my 20-year-old 'computerized' system, I went looking for a cost-efficient, integrated rental order-entry and reservation system from a supplier who was readily available for support, if I needed it. I have found all this with URIM."
> – Gord Robinson, WeRentIt

With URIM in place, your business will still be a hive of activity. But all activity will be focused on meeting and exceeding customer expectations, generating repeat business and growing your business. Use URIM to:

- Become more organized and productive, better manage workload and keep the customer satisfied
- Reserve inventory for specific time periods
- Receive alerts if you are about to over-book items
- Reserve any special equipment needed for set up
- Produce quotes without reserving inventory
- Convert quotes into orders with a "one-button click"
- Enter separate billing and shipping addresses on forms
- Confirm and send quotes and orders by email
- Print delivery and pick-up forms to expedite delivery
- Better manage receivables and analyze sales
- Include tax exemptions and discounts on invoices
- Calculate overall sales automatically

Free Taste of Rental Manager: Download Demo

Build Your Hive: Purchase URIM

URIM: Getting Started [Note: Takes reader to landing page]

In short, the kind of thinking that you put into print DRM material goes into your web-based DRM landing page:

- What do people need to know before they take the action that you want them to take?

- How can you build trust and confidence?

- What kind of incentive can you offer to entice them to take action while they are on the site?

When you write for the web, you want to make it as easy as possible for readers to scan and absorb your copy. That means writing shorter sentences and paragraphs, using bold headers and bullet points when and where appropriate. (These same principles can be applied to print-based DRM brochures.)

Let's look at part of another landing page, below, for media interview training. It puts a call to action for a free report three paragraphs into the landing page. Putting a call to action close to the top of the page is a common landing page tactic, especially when you don't have a call to action at the top of the page. The free report includes practical information the reader can use, more information about the training offered and contact information. The free report call to action on the landing page does not interfere with the overall flow of the copy (again, design and layout is as critical as the writing of copy here). Of course, the free offer is repeated at the end of the landing page as well, along with relevant contact information.

Are you ready for your interview?

You never know when a reporter will call. So be prepared. Paul Lima can have you ready in one interactive session.

Are you seeking media attention? Are journalists seeking you? Either way, you need to be prepared for interviews with journalists, because they are prepared to interview you.

Why be prepared?

It's the information age and every executive, manager, corporate spokesperson and business owner should be able to condense news, financial data, product information and other announcements into brief, convincing messages—expressed in an articulate, memorable manner.

When it comes to getting your organization's message out to the public—customers, shareholders, sponsors, donors and other stakeholders—knowing how to talk to journalists and interact effectively with the media is essential. What you say and how you say it can have a lasting impact on your business because the media helps Canadians form opinions.

> **Request your FREE** *Are You Ready for Your Interview* report today. The report includes practical advice to help you prepare for interviews with reporters. Email info@paullima.com with "Media Interview Report" in the subject line.

The key to successful interviews?

Developing and delivering a message that is simple, interesting and newsy is key to successful interviews. In most interviews, you should stick to several carefully crafted key messages and draw on a couple supporting points and examples. You should judiciously repeat key messages for emphasis, while answering questions. Paul Lima's half-day or full-day media interview training seminars will show you how to do just that.

> "We have been using Paul Lima for media training for every client at Infinity PR. Paul's training is insightful and our clients take away great learning from the sessions. All of our clients have been extremely happy with the training." – Alan McLaren, Infinity PR

The landing page copy goes on to describe how media training seminars can help you prepare for media interviews in one interactive session, in person or over the phone (which is how many interviews are conducted). It also includes another testimonial and a link to an article that describes how media interview training, coupled with effective PR, turned a book into a Canadian bestseller. Finally, it repeats the "request your free media interview training report" information and includes contact (phone and email) information.

The use of bold subheads, short paragraphs and indents for the testimonials (which you may not see in ebook versions of this book) all make the copy easy to scan. There is no incentive to "buy" media training; however, the call to action for the free report is clearly stated, as is the contact information. The free report would be used to demonstrate the trainer's knowledge about media interviews and would include contact information and a call to action.

Again, this approach puts a call to action close to up front, but notice it's for the free report. People seldom buy media interview training on a whim, so the trainer (me, in this instance) sells his credibility and the need for training before he sells the actual training—a conscious choice, which is what you need to make.

In summary, when writing for the web, you want copy that:

- is clear, concise, focused, well written and easy to scan and absorb

- speaks to a clearly defined target market

- conveys your purpose and supports your purpose

- presents a clear call to action and, if appropriate, an incentive to act

Generally, as has been indicated, web copy should be more concise and shorter than print-based writing; however, you still need to capture attention, hold interest, influence attitude and ask for action. In short, web copy should not be so short that it skips any of those steps. It should also not be so concise that it leaves out important information that the reader requires before deciding to act.

Now What?

Now pick a product or service that you want to promote, perhaps one for which you wrote a Google ad. Try to apply what we have gone over here and create a website landing page. Once again, think hook, line and sinker. However, keep in mind that the prospect has used keywords to find you. He/she is pre-qualified—so put your call to action up-front, if it makes sense to the product and target audience. Don't forget to use the hotlink advantage when appropriate. At the same time, if you feel all your copy should be on one page, I have no problem with that. Think it through and make a conscious decision—one that will help you best achieve your purpose. Finally, remember that your landing page appears on the web, so all the web-writing principles we have gone over apply.

Chapter 16: Search Engine Optimization

Search Engine Optimization (SEO) is the process of making website content accessible to search engines and improving its rank in search engine listings when people search for the type of information, goods and/or services that you offer from your website. That leads to the question: How do you go about optimizing your site for the highest possible search engine rank?

What is Content?

For the purpose of websites and SEO, content includes any text that the search engine robots ('bots) can capture. Images (graphics), animation and Flash are not content. In other words, words created in a graphics program and displayed on your website are not content.

How do you know what content is applicable to SEO? Go to a web page (in your web browser) and click on:

Edit > Select All > Edit, Copy

Then open Notepad (not Word or WordPerfect!) and click on:

Edit > Paste

Anything you see in Notepad (which cannot display graphic images) is editable text or content. And the search engine 'bots love content

Why Optimize?

Since the web is being used for product research and comparison, comparison pricing, and to close sales, companies are doing their best to attract visitors to their websites. However, there are hundreds of millions of pages on the web, all vying for attention. While behemoth corporations such as Coke, Microsoft and Nike can draw audiences to their websites with the weight of their brand and marketing muscle, small and medium businesses draw most of their online traffic through search engines.

To show up in search engines results, a website must be submitted to the search engine, or found and indexed by search engine 'bots. It can take anywhere from several days to several months or longer to index a website. Proper SEO helps speed up the process.

To rank high in search engine results, the site must be optimized for relevant search terms. When it comes to search results, rank matters. Traffic drops significantly by rank, according to the Atlas Institute, the research arm of Atlas DMT, an advertising technology provider. The first site listed in search engine results receives three times the hits of the fifth site; the first 10 sites (generally the first page of results) are visited 78% more often than sites listed 11th to 30th.

Keywords are Key

Before you begin to optimize a website for the best possible search engine results, you need to define your keywords and phrases—the words and phrases prospective customers will enter into search engines when looking for the kind of product or services you sell (or the causes you support, the political stance you take or the hobby you enjoy).

Once you have defined those keywords:

Use a consistent, text-based site navigation menu that incorporates your keywords. Search engines like text (content). They use site content when determining site relevancy to search terms. The 'bots the search engines send out to find websites cannot read images, so your navigational menu should ideally be composed of text. If it is composed of images (many *words* on the web are actually graphic images that spell them out), then make sure you use *alt tags* (see below).

Include keyword text tags (alt tags) with graphics (or a graphics-based navigation menu). Every image on a website has a name (something.jpg or imagename.gif and so on.). HTML code is used to display an image in a browser page (HTML code goes beyond the scope of this book). The images mean nothing to the 'bots; however, if you add an *alt tag* to your HTML code, then you are adding readable content that the 'bots can use.

Note: Have you ever placed your cursor over an image and seen one of those little yellow flags with text? If so, your browser is set to display alt tags and the website designer used alt tags. The 'bots pick up the alt tag as text. So your alt tag should be something like "world's greatest freelance writer"—only substitute your keywords or phrases for mine.

Combine keyword text with Flash. The 'bots cannot read Flash animation pages, so make sure you include some keyword text on a Flash-based website page.

Build a text site map, an uber-navigational page, one that includes links to every page on your site. Link to your site map from your home page so the 'bots that land on your home page can find your site map. Your site map will help the 'bots find and index every page on your site.

Write meta tags. Meta tags are embedded in HTML code and they can contain your keywords. Three basic meta tags are particularly meaningful: Title, Description and Content. Only the title tag is seen by visitors. The title meta tag displays the name of each website page in the visitor's web browser. You can change the title meta tag on each page to reflect the products, services or information on each page. You can also change the description and content meta tags, but unless each page or your site changes dramatically—golf shoes versus bridal shoes—you will most likely use one set of description and content meta tags.

Note: Although not as anywhere as important to rank as they were in the pre-Google days, meta tags are read by all search engines and may be used to display information about your site in search engine results. If your meta tags are focused on your keywords, if they are all thematically related and are in sync with the content on your site, the search engine believes your site is about what it says it is about and it pays greater attention to your meta tags when ranking your site.

Use keywords in all your site content. Every descriptive paragraph on your site should include keywords or phrases. Make sure links include them too. Instead of using a link that says "Click here for information on our products" use one that includes your keywords, such as "Click here for information on RubberBand's super-durable, superior elastic rubber bands that stretch to infinity and beyond." I am ex-aggerating, but I think you see the difference.

Beg, borrow and barter reciprocal links. When determining Page rank, most search engines look at *Link Popularity* or the number of links that point to your site (from other sites). For instance, using links from Site A to Site B as a vote by Site A for Site B, Google's PageRank system determines the value of sites. Google and other search engines see links to a site as a validation of the site. The greater the validation, the higher a site shows up in search engine results (as long as it is also well optimized for keyword searches). So if you can get non-competitive sites—especially if they are industry-related sites—linking to your site, you can improve your search engine results.

Note: Do not build fake sites with keywords and create links from them to your main site. That is known as SEO spamming. If the 'bots pick up on this, and they will, your sites will be delisted from the search engine.

Consider blogging. 'Bots like content related to your search terms and they like links to your site. A blog, if it pertains to your products, services, causes, issues will contain related keywords. If others read your blog (how you get them to do that goes beyond the scope of this book) and like what they read, they will link to your blog. So there you go: content and links! Just what you need.

Submit your site to search engines. While the 'bots may find you if you have links to your site, you should not sit back and wait. Instead, visit the major search engines and find out how to submit your site.

Chapter 17: Social Media

At the risk of sounding like a broken record, when it comes to writing anything, including social media content such as tweets, LinkedIn and Facebook posts, blog posts or other content, you want to know your purpose (why you are writing, what you hope to achieve), your target reader, the word count (or in some cases, such as Twitter, the character count), format you should follow and any call to action you might want to make.

You do your research, which could be internal, or external, outline your document keeping the above points in mind, and then you write.

"Even for a 140-character tweet?" I can hear you asking.

My answer, or I wouldn't be sounding like a broken record, is, as always, "Yes."

You might spend less time on all of the above if you are tweeting, but answer me this: Would you write a tweet without knowing why you want to write it? Would you tweet—and here I am talking business—without knowing who you were targeting and why? Would you produce those 140 characters (or less) without thinking about who you are or whom you represent and your relationship with your target reader? Would you send your tweet into cyberspace without knowing what, if anything, you hoped the reader would do? (I am not saying you have to have a call to action in mind when you tweet; I am saying you should think about whether or not you want to include one.)

When you tweet, you want to think about all that. Otherwise, why are you tweeting? What are you trying to accomplish?

But more on what you want to say and how you might say it in a bit.

What is Social Media?

Social media content, often called user-generated content, includes websites such as LinkedIn, Facebook and blogs, as well as Twitter, online discussion forums and so on. YouTube, for instance, is a video-based social media site that we will mention. And there are many new and developing social media sites, such as Google+, Google's attempt to emulate Facebook, Pinterest, an online site where you can collect and organize things that inspire you, and many, many others.

This chapter includes an overview of social media in general and of LinkedIn, Facebook and Twitter in particular, with a passing glance at YouTube. In the next chapter, we go blogging.

Social Media Stats

Social media has grown faster than any other media to date. For instance, it took radio thirty eight years to reach fifty million listeners. It took TV thirteen years to reach fifty million viewers. The Internet hit fifty million surfers in four years. Facebook hit two hundred million users in less than a year and has now surpassed one billion users. To put the growth of social media into context, social media has overtaken porn as the number one activity on the web, so you know there are many, many people engaged in social media.

Facebook

All of Facebook's users are on the Internet, but not all Internet users are on Facebook; however, Facebook users congregate in one place—on Facebook. Because so many people are on Facebook, advertisers want to be there too.

Facebook users tend to chat and interact socially, but the site is used for promotional purposes because it has so many subscribers. Companies run ads on Facebook and many companies have Facebook sites. In fact, some business-to-consumer companies often don't include their corporate website in ads; instead, they include their Facebook address (www.facebook.com/company-name) and try to drive Facebook members to their Facebook pages. They hope visitors will read their promotional messages and view videos, "like" their page, engage in discussions and post positive comments, enter contests, and interact in other ways the company initiates. In other words, they try to make their Facebook page "sticky"—to get visitors there, keep visitors there, and to keep them coming back.

When it comes to writing for Facebook, there are several things you can do, such as write Facebook ads, posts on your social site or posts on a company site. Ads on social sites are not part of this book, but reread the chapter on Google ads. The same principles apply. You just have to be aware of the line, word and/or character count restrictions. We will, however, take a moment and look at posts on company Facebook sites.

Take the Dove Facebook page, for example. Dove has one million Facebook fans. On its Facebook home page (www.facebook.com/dove), the company has copy, images and links to videos. While some of the material promotes products, some of it promotes causes that the company supports.

On its Facebook wall, Dove starts with an introduction to the company. (Note: things change rapidly online, so they may not appear as I have written about them here.) Now Dove is a huge company and it could probably fill a page talking about itself. But would readers read a long missive about Dove on Facebook? Probably not. Here is what Dove has on its wall:

Dove is committed to helping all women realize their personal beauty potential by creating products that deliver real care. Visit www.dove.ca for more information.

Short and sweet, no? Notice that it is not selling, at least not overtly, and that its target market—women—is clearly identified. Also notice that if you want to read a whole lot more about Dove, there is a link to its website. So while there is no hard-sell call to action, the reader can take action if she wants to know more by clicking on the link. In this way, Dove extends the life of its Facebook introduction for those who want more.

I happen to be writing this information about Dove on International Women's Day (IWD). Who is Dove's target audience? Women. That we know. So it's no surprise that Dove has information on its Facebook page today that pertains to IWD:

Want to do something to celebrate International Women's Day? Join us and help women around the world feel more beautiful by taking over negative ads! http://on.fb.me/ZlqmJq

The content reinforces Dove's brand and position in the market as a company that is committed to creating a positive image for women. In short, notice how the IWD blurb relates directly to the content and tone of the opening blurb on the page. This is called focusing on a message. The link at the end of the IWD blurb extends the message, for those interested in knowing more.

Here is part of Dove's Facebook mission statement:

Dove on Facebook is about promoting positive self-esteem and
helping women feel good about their unique inner and outer beauty.…

Is it fair to say that, over these three posts, we have a theme and we are stick-
ing to it? So even when you are writing short, you might be writing a lot and you want
to know who you are writing for, what you want to say and why, and any action you
want the reader to take. And you then want to focus on and repeat your theme to the
extent it makes sense to the reader.

Finally, on its Facebook wall, where interactive dialogues take place, Dove
initiates the discussion with posts like this:

Do you have sensitive skin? Has your Dermatologist or Doctor ever
recommended using Dove Sensitive Skin?

Visitors can "like" the message or respond to it, such as this reply from Alicia:

I've been devoted to Dove for over 30 years. WON'T use anything
else. The sensitive skin product is awesome! Thanks.

While there is room for a writer to produce Facebook promotions, user-
generated comments represent terrific word-of-mouth and they are important: 78% of
social media users trust peer reviews; 14% of TV watchers trust ads. So sometimes the
goal of the writer is to write posts that generate positive comments on social media
sites. And yes, some companies cheat. They have been accused of planting positive
comments on various social media sites. If that trend continues, trust will diminish.
While companies that use social media need to drive their agenda, they don't want to
cause people to feel that they are being manipulated—or the social media network will
call companies out and generate negative publicity.

LinkedIn

LinkedIn is the world's largest business-to-business (and professional-to-
professional) social media network, with over two hundred and fifty million members
and growing. LinkedIn members do things such as:

- Connect with contacts in their industry

- Boost brand awareness

- Showcase their knowledge by exchanging ideas, insights and opportunities with professionals in their industry or target market

On LinkedIn, you can set up company profiles and personal profiles for employees who join the site. Individual and corporate profiles on LinkedIn should be professionally written and reflect any key messages a company wants to convey about itself and its products, services and support. In other words, when writing profiles for LinkedIn you want to follow the writing process so that your writing is as concise and focused and targeted as possible.

Many people join LinkedIn, connect with others or accept invitations to connect, and then do nothing. One way, however, to raise a personal or corporate profile, and build brand awareness, is to participate in discussion groups on LinkedIn. While finding and joining various discussion groups goes beyond the scope of this book, I will say that LinkedIn makes it easy to do. The key, once you join (or start) a group, is to participate in an open manner that is not overtly promotional.

As a discussion forum group member you can post relevant questions, answer questions posted by others or comment on answers others give. Posting questions about issues or problems can be a good way to get discussions going. At the same time, answering questions can be an excellent way to demonstrate your knowledge about issues and situations. Most groups are moderated, which is good because it minimizes spam posts and ensures a degree of decorum.

Participating on discussion boards, where your target market might hang out discussing industry-related issues, involves writing. And before one posts to a discussion forum on behalf of the company they work for, they should know what impression they want to make and how to best make it. If an issue is particularly important, the person posting a response might want to get a copywriter or editor to review and edit a message before it is posted.

If I work in your sector and I post a question pertaining to a sector problem, issue or opportunity, do I want you to blow your horn about how great your products and services are, or do I want you to offer concrete and useful information? I presume you'd say the latter. And if I offer concrete and useful information—well-written and logically structured replies—you just might, at some point down the road, investigate my products or services. How will you know where to find me? In the signature that I end my post with, of course.

I don't try to sell my services when I participate in business-related discussion forums. But if anyone is interested in contacting me or visiting my website, they don't have to look far, because all the information they'd need is in my signature:

Regards,
Paul Lima
Freelance Writer & Business-Writing Trainer
(416) 628-6005; www.paullima.com

Companies can advertise on LinkedIn, as they can on Facebook. If they chose to do so, all the principles addressed in this book and my advertising copywriting book, *Copywriting that Works*, come into play. Ads on LinkedIn, which are similar to ads on Facebook, Google and other search engines, should capture the attention of a defined target market and motivate people to click. When ads are clicked on, they should lead to a landing page, not a corporate home page. The landing page, as we have discussed, should encourage visitors to take a specific action—be it buy, donate, ask for a sales representative to call, complete a survey, support a cause, sign a petition, and so on.

Twitter

Twitter has been defined as the social media networking site for those who do not have many real friends and require random strangers to know minute details of their daily lives. However, Twitter is not used solely for short (maximum 140 characters) personal comments. People comment on all sorts of topics—personal life, social situations, causes and issues, politics, celebrity gossip, products and services, and so on.

Twitter has over five hundred million users, although many subscribers seldom tweet and don't regularly read tweets of those they follow, or they tweet a lot when they join and then the novelty wears off.

If you tweet, as posting a message on Twitter is called, nobody receives what you have to say unless they choose to follow you. How to gain Twitter followers goes beyond the scope of this book but allow me to quickly point out one way: look for and follow people who tweet about topics of interest to you or your company. The people you follow can then choose to follow you. You can also follow the followers of the person you chose to follow. Again, they may choose to follow you. (There are other ways to build your followers; a quick Google search on the topic will reveal a number of articles that may be of interest.)

So do I tweet?

Absolutely. I use Twitter to help sell my books and my writing and training services. You might be able to easily imagine promotional tweets that I might write, but my followers don't really want to read promotions about Paul Lima. Hence, I blog as well, and then use tweets to drive people to practical information on my blog (see Circle of Social Media below). Here are a couple of tweet examples:

The anatomy of writing a speech or presentation: http://website-address-here

5 Questions to ask before you write your non-fiction book: http://website-address-here

Introduction to "Unblock Writer's Block" now online: http://website-address-here

The Case Study case study: A case study on why to add case studies to your website: http://website-address-here

So let's breakdown some of those tweets? Do we see all five Ws? Not overtly, but the most important Ws are there. That is why I suggest that you think about them before you tweet, and consciously choose what to say. For instance, what do we have in this tweet: The anatomy of writing a speech or presentation: http://website-address-here? We have the what. But notice that in the what we have an appeal to the who, speech writers. We also have the call to action, which is also our where, as in where a person can read this anatomy. We don't have who wrote it. Or do we? The tweet reader can see a picture of, and the name of, the person who is tweeting. The only thing missing is the when, and by implication the tweeter is saying, "Click on this now." If you have a twitter account and follow a number of people, you know how quickly those tweets can scroll by. We don't really have a why, but presumably if you are the target audience, you will want to read this (what's in it for me or why should I read this) to help you with your speech writing.

How about the last tweet: The Case Study case study: A case study on why to add case studies to your website: http://website-address-here? I suspect you will see a very similar analysis. We know who is tweeting and who this appeals to: someone, presumably in a marketing or promotion position, who is responsible for website content. Our what is a case study on why to use case studies on websites. Where? You have a website address that will take you there. When? Again, there is no specific when, but we can presume we want the reader to click when he or she this. If we were promoting a concert, we could have the date. What about the why? That question will be answered when you read the tweet. Conversely, I suspect you can imagine a tweet that said something about boosting inquiries or even boosting sales by using case studies on your website. Also, seldom would someone tweet once about a topic like this, so there will be opportunities to use more overt whys in different tweets.

I even tweet testimonials for my work, as in this example:

"Excellent exercises for overcoming writer's block. Don't sit down without it!" – Tony Levelle, freelance writer – http://ow.ly/jm7wK

These tweets don't mean that you have to blog to tweet. It means you have to have something worth saying—something that your Twitter followers want to read and will find useful, interesting and/or entertaining. Again, using our concert example, we could send out some teaser tweets about a singer coming to New York. But at some point, we'd send out tweets with links to Ticketmaster or some other online ticket ordering site. There the visitor can take action—buy tickets. That's like providing a link to a blog post that provides more information and provides a link to a site where the reader can buy the product, make a donation, sign a petition or take some other action. In short, all this must be thought through (*planned*) before you begin to tweet.

With that in mind, should companies join Twitter? There is only so much companies can do; however, if a company feels its target market is on Twitter, then it should consider tweeting. Companies can use Twitter to build brand awareness by tweeting about existing and new products and services. They can also use tweets to drive traffic to their websites, Facebook pages and blogs (see circle of social media below).

Anatomy of a Tweet

When it comes to a closer look at the anatomy of a tweet, there is no one tweet style fits all. Again, by way of broken record, what you tweet depends (at minimum) on your purpose, target reader and any action you want the reader to take—all in no more than 140 characters.

Analysts have, however, studied the components of effective tweets and have found some common denominators that you will want to keep in mind when tweeting.

Include links: tweets that included links were three times more prevalent in retweets than those without. In other words, readers of tweets appreciate it when you complete the circle of social media.

Opt for timely news when possible: tweets mentioning timely news or events were the most shared. It may not always be possible to share news. But there is good news beyond newsy tweets. The next most shared tweets were instructional in nature (followed by entertainment, opinion, products and small talk).

Share tech news (or maybe mention a celebrity): Again, this won't apply to everyone, but researchers at UCLA said tweets about tech news were the often shared. Health news and "fun stuff" were number two and three in terms of popularity.

Use hash tags in your tweets: If you are tweeting about something timely, or if you are tweeting about something that others who may not be following you could be interested in, use hash tags (the # symbol) beside key words in your tweets. For instance, when I tweet about writing or the business of freelance writing, I hash tag words like #writing and #freelance. My daughter works as a writer on a web series, Versus Valerie, and when people who promote the series tweet about it, they use the hash tag #VersusValerie. Hash tags make it easy for people interested in the topic to search for and find tweets on the subject.

Use "you" instead of "I": Among the words most commonly found in heavily shared tweets are "you," "Twitter," "please," "retweet," "post" and "check out." **Note:** asking someone to "please retweet" is a bit of a tacky practice you might want to avoid.

Circle of Social Media

Positive cyber word of mouth can help spread your message and drive traffic to a website using what I call "the circle of social media."

For instance, a company can announce a contest on its website and/or in its blog. It can then use Facebook, LinkedIn, Twitter and other social media to promote the contest. In its promotions it would, of course, include a link to the contest page on its website or blog. That would drive traffic to the contest. Also, if the company tweets about the contest and its followers retweet the tweet, more people will get to read about the contest and click through for details.

When people click on links in social media posts, they complete the circle of social media, going from the post to a website or blog for more information.

Companies can use the circle of social media, as can individuals. As you know, I am a freelance writer, author and writing trainer. While my website, paullima-.com, reflects that, my blog, http://sixfigurefreelancer.wordpress.com/, on the other hand, is primarily (not exclusively) used to promote my books on writing and the business of freelance writing. When I create a new blog post, I post the title of the post and its website address on Facebook, LinkedIn, Google+ and Twitter. That helps drive traffic to my blog post, which contains links to where people can purchase my books (if so inspired by my blog post). And the circle of social media is complete.

My hope is that the informative blog post will raise my profile and make me seem like a credible author, as well as spur people to like and repeat my messages. That, I hope, will drive additional traffic to my blog and help spur the sale of my books.

YouTube and Other Social Media

Most **YouTube** users create and post funny, odd or quirky videos on YouTube, or post social commentaries on a variety of topics; however, many companies and individuals, such as musicians and authors, post promotional videos on the site.

Once a video has been posted on YouTube, it can be embedded in a website or blog or on Facebook. The website address can also be added to posts on LinkedIn and Twitter. Again, the goal is to use social media (writing) to drive viewers to the promotional video and to create buzz about it.

While Lady Gaga (or her recording company) can post a Lady Gaga music video on YouTube and have over a million people view in a matter of days, companies should not expect to reach a mass audience. And why would they want to? For the most part, companies want to reach their target markets. If a video is well made (well written and well produced) and contains valuable and/or informative information, it can attract an appropriate viewership—members of the identified target market. And if viewers like it, they can embed it in blogs and on Facebook and post links to it on LinkedIn and Twitter. So YouTube can be a viable promotion vehicle.

There are many other social media sites, too many to list here. But here are several that might be of interest to companies.

Tumblr is a site that lets you share anything—text, photos, quotes, links, music and videos—from your browser, phone, desktop, email, or wherever you happen to be.

Flickr is an online photo management and sharing application. The site has two main goals: to help people make their photos available to a select or mass audience, and to enable new ways of organizing photos and video. Companies can use Flickr but, as with any marketing, they should have a concrete business reason— building brand or product awareness, raising profile, driving sales—before choosing to use the site.

Google+ is a social networking site from Google. Users can share links, photos, videos, status messages and comments organized in "conversations". (Since this book was published, Google has abandoned "Buzz" and now runs **Google+** as its social media site.)

There is a list of social media sites, and what they are about, on Wikipedia – http://en.wikipedia.org/wiki/List_of_social_networking_websites.

Wikipedia itself is a social media site, in that users generate the content on the site. In other words, companies can have Wikipedia entries on the site—entries that can be edited by anyone who has a Wikipedia account. And if people feel a Wikipedia entry is incorrect or offensive (and incorrect or offensive is in the eye of the beholder) they will alter the post.

Follow Paul on…

If you are interested in seeing how I use social media, you can connect with me in various places:

- Twitter: https://twitter.com/PaulWriterLima

- Facebook: www.facebook.com/paul.lima

- Facebook fan page: www.facebook.com/pages/Paul-Lima/183948319355?ref=nf

- My blog: http://sixfigurefreelancer.wordpress.com/

- LinkedIn: www.linkedin.com/profile/view?id=4128829&trk=tab_pro

- *How To Write A Non-Fiction Book In 60 Days* YouTube trailer: www.youtube.com/watch?v=ytmUI17gtgg

Chapter 18: Writing Blog Posts

Blogs are an online phenomena, with hundreds of millions of blogs out there. Even though, it must be added, many are "ghost blogs"—blogs that have been abandoned in cyberspace. Many blogs are frivolous and personal; indeed, some companies think blogs are only used by people who are interested in celebrity gossip or venting about some perceived injustice. In other words, there is a feeling that blogs are not used for business purposes. However, when it comes to blogging, you don't have to care what individuals are posting in their blogs. All you have to care about is *your* content and potential audience.

Blogs that present solid business, technical or industry information are read on a regular basis. Company blogs may not attract a mass consumer readership, but that is not the goal of such blogs. As with other promotions, company blogs should be set up to attract the attention of a defined target market, not a fractured mass audience.

There are many reasons why companies should blog and take a planned, systematic approach to producing useful, informative and compelling blog content that focuses on topics of interest to their target market. Blogs can boost the rank of a company's website in search engine results, help companies deepen their relationship with existing customers, engage new prospects and build their brand in the online universe.

Boost SEO

Since a website's rank in search results is determined by its relevance to specific search terms and by link popularity, blogs make sense.

As you can imagine, a company's blog posts would use the kind of keywords that its target audience might use if searching for information related to the company's products or services. If your target audience finds posts in your company blog interesting, informative and credible, they might post links on their blogs and websites to your blog posts. Over time, your company blog would use and repeat a variety of keywords and phrases relevant to your industry and would be linked to from a variety of other blogs and websites. This boosts your company's rank in search results and helps drive traffic to your blog, which can be (and should be) linked to your website.

Blogs that present interesting, informative and credible information capture the attention of a defined target audience, and they can keep readers coming back. If readers find the content of a blog interesting, informative and credible, they can subscribe to the blog. Whenever the blog is updated, the reader is notified and can click on a link to the blog and read the latest entry.

Imagine Your Target Market Seeking You

Imagine spending nothing but a bit of time to create compelling content about your company, your products and services, or trends and issues pertaining to your industry, and having people in your target market actively seeking out and reading this content. That is what blogs enable you to do.

Ironically, however, many companies do not blog, blog erratically or only post blatantly promotional notices in their blog. In short, they miss this simple, low-cost and effective marketing opportunity.

To attract and hold readers, you have to give your readers something they want to read—help them learn something important, work more effectively or productively, solve problems, save time or money, discover new opportunities or take advantage of existing opportunities. Also, to hold the interest of your audience, you need to blog on a regular basis. Regular blogging does not mean daily, as too much information can overwhelm readers. Blogging once a week seems to work for many companies, although some companies blog several times a week or a couple of times a month.

Build Relationships

Blogs can help business-to-business (B2B) and business-to-consumer (B2C) companies deepen their relationships with existing customers. People who buy products from companies, especially if they are complex ones, like to have their purchase reinforced. In other words, even after they buy, they like to read good news about the product—how it works and can be used. This kind of information helps reinforce their purchase decision. With their purchase decision reinforced, they are more likely to become repeat customers and more likely to tell others about their purchase. And, as most companies know, no marketing is more cost-effective than repeat business and no marketing is more effective than positive word of mouth.

Keep Content Short(ish)

When blogging, you want to make sure your blog posts are not too long, otherwise they will not be read all the way through. Length is relative based on the topic being addressed; however, effective blog posts tend to run two hundred to six hundred words in length. That does not mean they can't be longer on occasion, but they should not be much longer on a consistent basis. Or, on the other hand, if you have something lengthy to say, you can post a synopsis of the topic on your blog and link from your blog post to a web page or PDF. The most interested readers will click on the link (you should be able to measure click-throughs) and continue to read.

Just as every prospect who reads ads about a company's products will not buy, not every blog reader will click on links in blog posts to the company's website. However, the links are there for readers who want to know more. And knowing more is the first step prospects take before they buy.

Generating Blog Post Topics

Before you write a blog post, clearly decide on your topic, which segment of your target market the post will appeal to, and what problem or opportunity you will address. Your post should stay focused on that topic, segment and issue. This might mean some prospects will not be interested in particular posts; however, if you try to be everything to everybody in each post, you will end up being nothing to nobody.

With that in mind, create some big-picture subject areas that you can blog about, including industry trends, issues and opportunities, and specific issues and opportunities for various sectors of your target audience. Use clustering to help you come up with big picture topics. Once you have your big picture ideas, brainstorm blog-post topics under each big-picture subject. Within an hour or two, you can develop a number of blog post topics—topics that will be of interest to various segments of your target market.

Once you have developed the topics, create a schedule—a list of topics, the dates you will blog about each topic, and who within your company (or outside your company, such as industry analysts or customers) will write the blog posts. And make sure any post is well edited before it goes online.

Your blog post schedule will keep you on track so that your blog has a constant flow of new and compelling content, which will help hook readers and keep them coming back. Of course, as industry issues emerge, or if you produce new products/services or revamp existing ones, you can revise the schedule and make room to cover emerging issues or to blog about your new products or product updates. Beware, however, of making your blog content overly promotional.

While you can produce solid, simple and factual descriptions about your products, I suggest you go beyond such posts and blog about industry trends and issues (this is where brainstorming topics come into play) to demonstrate the extent to which you understand your industry. You can, of course, relate some of these issues to your products, but you don't always have to do that. Sometimes simply demonstrating an understanding of an issue or opportunity, without overt commercial overtones, helps build your standing in the industry.

How to Write Blog Posts

Blog posts generally have three sections—introduction, body and conclusion.

Introductory paragraph: The crucial part of any blog post is the introductory paragraph. It should be no more than a couple of lines and should summarize what the post is about: after reading the first few lines, readers should know what the purpose of the post is and what they will learn or discover. That will entice readers to read on.

The W5 news article lead can be very helpful here. That doesn't mean you have to have every W in your opening paragraph. It does mean that you outline your Ws and determine which ones are most important in relation to your topic. Ensure you use them in your lead.

Body: Next comes the body of the post. Different points should always be separated by paragraphs and major topic shifts should have their own sub-heads. The sub-head, in conjunction with the first sentence of each paragraph or section, should spell out the topic of the paragraph or section and lure readers into continuing to read.

Because readers scan or browse when they read online content, you'll want to keep your paragraphs short to avoid large, intimidating chunks of text. If it makes sense, add graphics to illustrate points, but don't add frivolous graphics for the sake of having images in your post.

If you want to convey a series of points, consider using bulleted or numbered lists because they are easier to scan and absorb than full paragraphs.

Conclusion: Finally, end your blog post with a conclusion or summary paragraph, a round-up of what you've been writing about, a list of recommendations or what action the reader might.

If you go to my Hockey Night on Ossington Avenue blog post (http://-sixfigurefreelancer.wordpress.com/2013/12/31/hockey-night-on-ossington-avenue), you would say that I have not followed my advice. But then the blog post is actually a short story, so it comes as no surprise that the post does not follow the advice I have outlined here. However, look at the opening to *SEO in Non-fiction Book Titles can Boost Sales* (online at http://sixfigurefreelancer.wordpress.com/2013/12/12/seo-in-non-fiction-book-titles-can-boost-sales). Allow me to present it to you here:

I can't believe how well *How to Write a Non-fiction Book in 60 Days* and several other of my books on writing and freelance writing continue to sell on Amazon, in the US and the UK, as print and Kindle books. I don't do a lot of promotion, other than using some social media. The books are selling in numbers greater than my promotional efforts merit. It took me a while to figure out why, but it makes so much sense.

Let's deconstruct the W5:

Who: I (Paul Lima, the blogger)

What: can't believe how well *How to Write a Non-fiction Book in 60 Days* and several other of my books on writing and freelance writing continue to sell … The books are selling in numbers greater than my promotional efforts merit.

Where: on Amazon, in the US and the UK, as print and Kindle books

When: continue to (now)

Why: It took me a while to figure out why, but it makes so much sense. (In other words, this is such a big point that most of the rest of the blog post will be devoted to it.)

Let's look at a post from Geosoft, a geology software development company. Below are the opening two paragraphs from 3D Earth Modelling in the Cloud: The Geosoft VOXI development story:

Released in April, 2012, Geosoft's VOXI Earth Modelling service gives exploration geophysicists the ability to convert magnetic and gravity data directly into useful 3D Earth models that can be integrated with other 3D exploration data.

Creating the cloud-based VOXI inversion service took us over three years, and required the work of 29 people on a number of development teams. This is the story of how we did it.

Deconstructing it, we see:

Who: Geosoft

What: VOXI Earth Modelling service

Where: cloud-based

When: Released in April, 2012,

Why: gives exploration geophysicists the ability to convert magnetic and gravity data directly into useful 3D Earth models that can be integrated with other 3D exploration data

In short, if you outline your W5 before you write—and it can take some thinking, planning and plain old work to do so—you are far more likely to speak to your target audience in a clear, concise and focused manner.

Blog Headlines: Accurately Reflect Content

When creating a headline or title for your blog post, you don't need to be overly creative. In fact, the more direct you are, the better the headline will be. For instance, "What happens when we drain Canada dry?" might make for a cute and effective newspaper headline, one that will cause curious readers to read the article when they stumble upon the headline. But it makes for a not so good blog headline for an article pertaining to the ecological consequences of diminishing water resources in Canada.

In other words, you want your blog headline to accurately reflect the content of your article. When your article is picked up by search engines, they will serve up your headline as the link to the blog post based on key words used for searches. How many people would search for "What happens when we drain Canada dry?" If somebody included "Canada Dry" in a search, they would most likely be looking for information on the soda pop by the same name. People interested in environmental issues might, however, search for "ecological consequences" or "diminishing water resources" and cause the search engine to serve up a link to an article with those words in the title.

So don't try to write cute blog headlines; write headlines that accurately reflect the content of your blog post. Or combine a practical approach with something cute, using your friend, the colon, as in the following:

- What happens when we drain Canada dry: ecological consequences of diminishing water resources

- How to write an effective blog headline: sexy doesn't always cut it

- Gotcha: How using W5 headlines and leads captures attention of readers

I think you get the point. Be practical. Doesn't mean you can't have any fun, but make sure you are practical if you want people to find your blog post using search engines. If you are driving hordes of traffic to your site using other promotional means, be as sexy crazy as you want to be.

Putting Social Media Theory into Practice

By way of quick review, we've looked at Facebook, LinkedIn, Twitter, blogging and the circle of social media. Now it's time to put into practice the theory you've been reading about.

I could give you a series of exercises, but ideally the social media exercise you do should be based on your interests, be it the products or services you sell, the causes you support, or the products and services the company you work for sells.

With that in mind, engage in the circle of social media. Write a blog post and try to drive traffic to it. Before you write, I want you to do a few things:

- Pick a product, service, cause, company, issue you'd like to write about.

- Jot down who you are in relation to the above (you might be a business owner, an employee, an interested third party and so on).

- Briefly describe your target reader, based on demographics (age, gender, income and so on), lifestyle, sector the reader works in, position within a company, type and size of company, and so on.

- In one sentence (that may be longer than a tweet), describe your writing purpose.

- Describe any action you hope a reader might take.

- Jot down a key word or phrase related to product, service, cause, company, issue you'd like to write about.

- Cluster that word or phrase.

Once you have completed the above process, here's what you do:

- Write a blog post on the issue (two hundred to six hundred words should do). Should your blog post include links to any websites? If so, make sure you include them. Also, make sure you give your blog post a practical title.

- Write three tweets related to the blog post. One can simply be the title of the post. Make sure you include your blog post address. (Feel free to make one up if you don't actually have a blog.) Remember, the address is part of your 140 tweet characters. If your address is long, you can shorten it here: http://tinyurl.com/. **Note:** some tweet applications, such as HootSuite and TweetDeck automatically shorten website addresses.

- Write a short blurb, a summary as it were, of your blog post for Facebook and LinkedIn. Keep it to no more than twenty-five or so words; include your blog post address.

Chapter 19: Writing Sentences

In the beginning was the word. It was quickly followed by the sentence. Which, of course, was followed by the paragraph.

Do you know what the shortest sentence in the Bible is? Two words: *Jesus wept.* The sentence has a subject (*Jesus*) and a verb (*wept*). That is all a sentence needs to be complete. Where, however, is the subject in the following two-word sentence?

Do it!

The subject, *you*, in a command or imperative is understood. Everyone who hears the simple command *Do it!* understands it to mean **You** *do it*. Drop the *you*, start the sentence with the verb (to do), and the sentence packs a more powerful punch.

Without a subject (real or implied) and verb, you have a sentence fragment:

Because I.

Over there.

The officer.

However, look at the third sentence in this chapter:

Which, of course, was followed by the paragraph.

When you read it, did you notice that it was a sentence fragment? (Where is the subject?) Did it feel like a fragment when you read it? Even if it did, was it effective? Does it feel like a fragment now that you are reading it out of context?

Although sentence fragments can be used effectively, particularly in advertising, seldom will you use them in business writing. If they are not used appropriately—for a conscious effect or to emphasize a particular point—they can create disjointed writing and can cause miscommunication and confusion.

Part of your goal as a writer is to become aware of, and correct, sentence faults and other problems that can interfere with clear, concise communication. You do this when editing your work. In other words, don't get hung up on fixing errors as you write. That will thwart your writing efficiency. At the same time, if you follow the writing process, especially the creation of detailed outlines, you will bring greater clarity and focus to your writing and so have fewer revisions to make when editing.

While grammar and spelling count, this is not a book about grammar and spelling. With that in mind, I will not spend much time on particular sentence faults. We will, however, look at the active and passive voice. In addition, there are examples of how to construct effective sentences in this chapter. However, if grammar is a concern, look there are many books and websites (too many to mention) that can help you.

Active versus passive voice

Read the two passages below. What is different about them? What is similar?

The Highway Department is building a new bridge in River Hollow. The backhoe digs deep holes. The cement mixer pours in concrete to make the supports.

Carefully Carlton picks up steel girders with his crane and lays them across the supports.

Bulldozers push up the surrounding ground to make a road. The grading machine smoothes the slope, and the asphalt spreader pours down a layer of blacktop. Brian's steamroller comes last to smooth it flat and even. Dennis and Darlene haul away the extra dirt in their dump truck.

Research into new advertising promotions that could boost company sales was initiated by marketing last spring.

A list of primary media read by our target market was compiled by Susan McMillan. Creative ideas were produced by the copywriting department. A campaign was designed by Frank Myers, the art director, and was launched in the summer.

Encouraging have been the sales results to date.

Does the first passage remind you of a grade one reader? If you are old enough to have gone on adventures with Dick and Jane, it might remind you of those famous sentences that you read when you were first learning to read:

See Dick. See Jane. See Dick run. See Jane run. See Spot. See Spot run. Hear Spot bark.

The sentences in both passages above are clear and concise. But are they effective or are they boring and monotonous? Could you imagine reading an entire website or report with sentences written only like the ones in the passages above?

In the first passage, the simple sentences are written in the active voice, which can be used to create short, direct sentences. The second passage is written entirely in the passive voice, which makes for longer, more awkward sentences that distance the reader from who did what. While effective sentences are generally written in the active voice, effective writing requires a mix of active and passive voice, a mix of complex and simple sentences and the use of sentences of various lengths.

Active voice

In the active voice, the *subject* performs the action expressed in the **verb**. In other words, the subject acts, as in the examples below:

The dog **bit** the boy.

Terri **presented** her research at the conference.

We **received** your shipment two days late, which caused delays.

You **sent** the shipment two days late, which caused delays.

Scientists **will conduct** experiments to test the hypothesis.

Passive voice

In passive voice, the *subject* receives the action expressed by the **verb**. The agent performing the action may appear in a "by the..." phrase or may be omitted entirely.

The boy **was bitten** by *the dog.*

Research **was presented** by *Terri* at the conference.

Your payment *was received* two days late, which caused delays.

Experiments *will be conducted* to test the hypothesis.

Notice the agents committing the action are missing from the last two sentences. Here are the last two sentences with the "by the" agents included:

Your payment was received two days late by the accounting department, which caused delays.

Experiments will be conducted by the scientists to test the hypothesis.

Do you need "by the accounting department" or "by the scientists" in the above sentences? The sentences are grammatically correct without the agents. If, however, it was important for the reader to know that the accounting department did not receive the payments, or that scientists will conduct the experiments, then the agents should be included. If not, no problem leaving them out.

Leaving the scientists out of the second sentence puts the focus on the experiments and why they will be conducted. There is nothing wrong with this focus, if that is where you want to put it. In other words, where you put your emphasis or focus, and the voice you use, should be conscious decisions.

Having said that, you should know that the passive voice can create awkward sentences and cause readers to become confused. Sentences written in the active voice require fewer words than those written in the passive voice. This makes for writing that is more concise. In addition, sentences in the active voice are generally clearer and more direct than those in the passive voice.

The passive voice can allow writers to compose without using personal pronouns or names of people or groups (as with the scientists and accounting department sentences). This can help create the appearance of an objective, fact-based discourse. However, the passive voice can also be used to deflect blame or avoid responsibility, which is not always warranted, as in the following sentence:

Seeking to lay off workers without taking the blame, consultants were hired to break the bad news.

Who was seeking to lay off workers? The consultants? That's what it looks like. However, the CEO was more likely responsible. If that is the case, leaving out the agent creates a misleading sentence that avoids allocating proper responsibility. So let's use active voice and include the responsible party:

Seeking to lay off workers without taking the blame, the CEO hired consultants to break the bad news.

Being direct can be important. There are times, however, when being indirect is preferable. If there is no clear agent, then there is no clear blame, and sometimes it is necessary to point out a problem without pointing fingers, as in these examples:

Several mistakes were made before the trains collided.

The quota was not met last month, so monthly bonuses have been withheld.

In the train example: Imagine that a train collision is under review. It is obvious that the trains should not have collided. The spokesperson for the railway company cannot deny that a collision has occurred. However, the spokesperson cannot say who made mistakes that caused the collision until the accident review is completed. Instead, she resorts to the passive voice and leaves out the agent so she does not allocate blame. If she had included the agent, she might have said something like this:

Several mistakes were made by the eastbound engineer before the trains collided.

And if she had used the active voice, she might have said this:

The eastbound engineer made several mistakes before the trains collided.

In the quota example: The person making the announcement might know which person or department did not meet quota but has chosen not to say it publicly. Also, notice that the person making the announcement has not credited an individual—the CFO (chief financial officer) or a specific manager—for withholding bonuses. What we have here is the withholding of two agents and the double use of passive voice in one sentence but it is not necessarily doublespeak. You might call it politically sensitive communication. Put in the agents and what do you have?

The quota was not met last month by the western sales team, so monthly bonuses have been withheld by the CFO.

How does the western sales team feel? And what do people think about the CFO?

Choosing active or passive voice

Since the passive voice highlights what is acted upon rather than focusing on the agent performing the action, using it often makes sense when the agent performing the action is obvious, unknown or unimportant. It also makes sense when a writer wishes to postpone mentioning the agent until the last part of the sentence, or to avoid mentioning the agent. In the active voice, the agent or subject is important to, or integral to, the sentence.

In the examples below, the passive voice makes sense if the agent is less important than the action and what is acted upon. If the agent is important, one would use the active voice.

Active: The dispatcher notified police only minutes after three prisoners had escaped.

Passive: Police were notified only minutes after three prisoners had escaped.

If it is more important to know how long it took for the police to be notified (than it is to know who notified the police), the passive voice makes sense. If there was some question as to who notified the police, and if that was more important than how long it took for the police to be notified, the active voice would make sense.

What is more important in these sentences: the spruce budworm or the damage?

Active: The spruce budworm has irrevocably damaged vast expanses of Cape Breton forests.

Passive: Vast expanses of Cape Breton forests have been irrevocably damaged by the spruce budworm.

In the passive voice sentence, the emphasis is on the damage to the forests, not the cause of the damage. If, however, you wanted to warn people about the spruce budworm, the active voice would make more sense.

When choosing between the active and passive voice, what you want to do is keep the reader, your topic and your purpose in mind. Also, think about clarity and conciseness. In other words, make conscious decisions concerning the use of the active and passive voice and the inclusion or exclusion of the agent performing the action. However, beware of using the passive voice to mask issues that should be addressed and don't overuse the passive voice.

Convert passive to active

Take a moment and convert the passive voice sentences below to active voice. If you are not sure that you have done it correctly, set grammar checker in Word or your word processing software to flag passive constructions and grammar check your revised sentences. You can also look at the revised sentences in Appendix Three toward the end of the book.

The entrance exam was failed by more than one third of the applicants to the school.

The brakes were slammed on by her as the car sped downhill.

Your bicycle has been damaged.

(The agent has been omitted. Who did the damage? Edit the sentence as if you did and edit it as if a thief has damaged the bicycle.)

Action on the bill is being considered by the committee.

By then, the soundtrack will have been completely remixed by the sound engineers.

To satisfy the instructor's demands for legibility, the paper was written on a computer.

(Before revising this, ask: Who was satisfying the instructor? The paper? Or the person writing the paper? Then edit the sentence.)

Once you have converted passive sentences to active voice, continue to read.

How to construct a sentence

As I mentioned, this is not a grammar book. I want to take a moment, however, to review the foundation of the sentence. At minimum, the sentence requires a subject and a verb (action). In *I laughed*, *I* is the subject; *laughed* is the verb. But two-word sentences generally don't cut it in business writing. So let's review a sentence that includes a *subject*, a **verb** and a third component—the <u>object</u>.

The boy **kicked** <u>the soccer ball</u>.

The boy is our subject (the person who does the action). **Kicked** is the verb or action. <u>The soccer ball</u> is our object, that which receives the action. I call these three elements "the heart of the sentence." If you ever feel that your sentences are getting too complex, find the heart. Once you have the heart, you can expand your sentence logically and keep the meaning clear. For instance, where did the ball go when the boy kicked it?

The boy kicked the soccer ball through the window.

What happened to the window?

The boy kicked the soccer ball through the window, which shattered into a thousand pieces.

Tell me more about this boy:

The tall, thin, Caucasian boy kicked the soccer ball through the window, which shattered into a thousand pieces.

Do you see how our sentence is becoming more complex? It is easy to understand, however, because we can still identify the heart of the sentence. Now imagine that this action was committed by a criminal.

The tall, thin, armed and dangerous Caucasian boy kicked the soccer ball through the window, which shattered into a thousand pieces.

What happened next?

The tall, thin, armed and dangerous Caucasian boy kicked the soccer
ball through the window, which shattered into a thousand pieces, and
then he fled the scene.

Notice we now have two "hearts" combined. Let me simplify them for you:

The boy kicked the soccer ball through the window.

He fled the scene.

Two subjects, two verbs, two objects. One sentence. Meaning is still clear
because we let one heart beat, so to speak, and then the other. If you think sentences
are running away on you, identify your subject and verb and build from there. If you
have more than one subject and verb, identify each of them and determine how best
to let them beat. Joined or as two separate sentences. If the complex sentence feels
like it is unclear, separate the two hearts:

The tall, thin, armed and dangerous Caucasian boy kicked the soccer
ball through the window, which shattered into a thousand pieces.
Then he fled the scene.

Keep this in mind as you try the other writing exercises in this book and as
you write and edit your work.

Chapter 20: Constructing Paragraphs

A paragraph is a collection of sentences organized around a clearly defined topic. If you are writing a long document, each paragraph topic will be a subtopic of, or somehow related to, the subject of the document you are writing.

The paragraph performs three functions:

1. develops the unit of thought stated in the topic sentence

2. provides a logical break in the material

3. creates a visual break on the page, thus signaling a new topic

Generally, the paragraph starts with a topic sentence. Often, this topic sentence is an important outline point converted into a complete sentence, followed by your subtopic outline points. The topic sentence states the paragraph's main idea. The rest of the paragraph supports and develops the idea.

The topic sentence is often the first sentence in a paragraph because it tells the reader what the paragraph is about. However, the topic sentence can be used to end a paragraph—almost like a punch line. Occasionally, the topic sentence can be found in the middle of the paragraph. There would be some build up to the topic sentence, the topic sentence and then some support of the topic.

Topic at the beginning

Here is an example with the topic sentence at the beginning of each paragraph:

The cost of orientation, health and safety and customer service training for new Customer Service Representatives (CSRs) is significant. The organization must cover the price of classroom facilities, instructors and manuals, and must pay employees their full salary during the two-week training period.

If the company is to break even on its investment in training, employees must stay in the job for which they have been hired for at least one year, according to our analysis (see attached PDF). However, on average, CSRs leave the company within nine months of hiring. Not only is the company losing money on employee training, it is also paying exorbitant recruitment costs to fill each vacancy.

To increase the return on investment (ROI) for training new CSRs, the committee proposes that the following five recommendations be implemented:

1. Recommendation one....

2. Recommendation two....

3. Recommendation three....

4. Recommendation four....

5. Recommendation five....

Notice how the first sentence of the first paragraph establishes both the subject of the document as well as the topic of the paragraph: "The cost of... is significant." I suspect you could imagine this sentence being used to establish the topic in almost any paragraph dealing with cost issues, such as: *The cost of purchasing parts from our current supplier is significant.* In short, the sentence raises an issue, which creates expectations that the document will explain why the cost of whatever is significant and will most likely suggest how the issue can be resolved. The rest of the paragraph explains why the cost is significant and the document goes on to suggest how to solve the problem.

The opening sentence of the second paragraph tells us the circumstances that must occur if we are to solve the problem. "If the company is to break even on its investment in training, employees must stay in the job for which they have been hired for at least one year..."

Notice also how it refers to an attached PDF. It often makes sense to attach complex details to an email message. By attaching the PDF, the writer can move quickly from the problem to the solution while offering those who need more information, proof in the attached document.

Finally, notice how the third paragraph consists of a topic sentence and five points or the actions to be taken. (There will be more on when and why to use bullet points or numbered points later in this chapter.) The document does not say when to take the action nor does it request feedback to close the communication loop. Presumably, the action is suggested; the writers are sending this information to management. Management must decide on what to do and when to do it, not the writers, so the writers do not have to request that action be taken by a specific date.

Topic at the end

Here is an example with the topic sentence at the end of the paragraph:

Energy does more than simply make our lives more comfortable and convenient. If you wanted to reverse or stop economic progress, the surest way to do so would be to cut off the nation's oil resources. The country would plummet into the abyss of economic ruin. In short, our economy is energy-based.

Often—not always—opening paragraphs in blog posts, email messages, executive summaries of reports and other documents place the topic sentence at the end of the paragraph. This lets the writer set the stage with a few lines that build up to the topic or purpose of the document.

Your topic and purpose can be made clear in the first line of the first paragraph, the last line of the first paragraph or even part way through your first paragraph. The important thing is that, almost without exception, the reader needs to know what you are writing about (your topic) and why (your purpose) by the end of the opening paragraph.

Paragraph length

The length of each paragraph should aid the reader's understanding of the idea addressed. A series of very short paragraphs can indicate poor organization and underdeveloped thoughts. Too many long paragraphs, however, can fail to provide the reader with manageable subdivisions of thought. The occasional one-sentence paragraph is acceptable if it is used for effect or as a transition between paragraphs. One-sentence paragraphs are also acceptable in blog posts, on websites or in email messages.

With that in mind, read the "healthcare" paragraphs below. The paragraphs make up the executive summary from a report written by a financial analyst for a major bank. To help you into the paragraphs, here is the title of the report:

Focus on Healthcare: Are Canadians Missing an Opportunity?

Take a moment and think about the expectations that this title raises. Based on this title, what do you expect the report to focus on? Who is the audience for this report? Why do you think that? Once you've mulled over the above questions, read the executive summary:

ABC Research Co. appears to have put a greater emphasis on products that cater to the healthcare industry. ABC estimates the U.S. market for furniture in the healthcare industry to be about $1.7 billion. Most of the market is supplied by regional suppliers. The market is split 50/50 between traditional office furniture and clinical furniture. ABC indicated that the market is expected to probably grow by 50% over the next seven years, driven by an aging population and needed replacement of aging facilities. Expectations of ABC are that there will be a greater growth within the clinical segment of the furniture market. Although Canadian manufacturers have talked about focusing on end markets in the U.S. including government, education and healthcare, it appears that the U.S. manufacturers have made more significant investments in targeting the healthcare market, given the clinical products they are offering to complement their traditional office furniture products. Given the expected growth in the market, we wonder whether Canadian manufacturers should perhaps consider acquiring small U.S. suppliers with heavy healthcare exposure as a way to increase penetration into this segment.

Expectations met or dashed?

Were your expectations, based on the title, met or dashed? Did the paragraph start with (or end with) a topic sentence? Did the writing support (or build up to) the topic? At what point did it occur that this report was about the healthcare *furniture* industry? At what point did it occur that the issue is whether Canadian *furniture manufacturers* (not Canadians generally) were missing the opportunity to move into the American healthcare *furniture* market? What did you make of wiggle words— "appears," "probably," "wonder," "should," "perhaps," and so on? Do they create confidence? And what of the conclusion or recommendation? Is it as powerful as it could be?

What is the purpose of the report? Is it achieved? Does the writing capture the attention of readers, hold interest or influence attitudes? If so, does it do it well? Does it clearly let them know what action they should take based on the arguments presented?

Let's review the three functions of the paragraph:

1. develops the unit of thought stated in the topic sentence

2. provides a logical break in the material

3. creates a visual break on the page, thus signaling a new topic

Now turn back to the ABC executive summary. What is the topic? Can you even find a true topic sentence? Or are there several topics at work here in one paragraph? If so, is there a logical break in the material between topics? What is your opinion of the lack of visual breaks? Are there logical points in the document where they could occur?

When presented with this document, how did you, as the reader, feel? I admit that reading these paragraphs is not as intimidating as reading Joseph Conrad (many of his paragraphs run on for pages) but my eyes scream for some visual relief every time I see this paragraph. Oh no, I think, if the entire document is going to look like this, then I don't want to read it.

Although this is not a book about layout and design, you need to know that the look of your document, particularly when it comes to writing for the web, can affect the attitude of readers toward your writing—even before they begin to read (or perhaps not read, if the writing looks like an impenetrable wall of words).

Paragraph exercise

With that in mind, take a shot at editing the executive summary presented above. Your goal is to read the summary, understand it, determine your purpose, organize it (create an outline) and revise it.

If you believe there is more than one topic addressed in the executive summary, turn it into multiple paragraphs. Rewrite sentences. Delete any information that does not advance your purpose. Create clear, concise writing that captures attention, holds interest, influences attitude and presents a clear call to action based on the facts. Oh, and feel free to give the report a new, more appropriate, title.

There is a sample of a revised executive summary in Appendix Three. However, tackle this exercise before you read it. Give your internal editor a good workout. And do not be concerned if your take on the revised summary is not the same as the example. No two people would produce the same revised document. The example is simply how one editor would turn the executive summary into a more concise, focused, well-structured document.

Once you have revised the executive summary, continue to read.

Bullet and numbered points

As we saw previously in this chapter, in the topic sentence example about "the cost of orientation, health and safety and customer service training," there are times when bullet point or numbered point sentences make sense.

Bullet and numbered points are easy to scan and absorb. They make sense when you are making a series of recommendations or when you are giving instructions—especially if the instructions must be performed sequentially. Look at the examples below. They are presented as conventional paragraphs and then as points, the first example numbered and the second example as bullets. In the first example, you have to take the steps in sequential order, hence the numbered points. In the second example, you should follow the points presented but you don't have to follow them sequentially, hence the bullet points.

Example I

For you to start juggling, you must do the following: first pick up A in your right hand, then you should pick up B in you left hand, and then you should toss A and then B into the air, catching A as you toss B and catching B and you toss A. Repeat continuously.

For you to start juggling, do the following:

1. pick up A in your right hand

2. pick up B in your left hand

3. toss A into the air

4. toss B into the air while catching A

5. toss A back into the air while catching B

6. repeat continuously

Example II

Three habits that improve health are getting eight hours of sleep each night, eating three balanced meals every day and exercising regularly.

Three habits that improve health are

- getting eight hours of sleep each night

- eating three balanced meals every day

- exercising regularly

The points convey the information in a manner that is easy to scan, absorb and understand. The shorter lines cause the eye to stop at the end of each point as the brain does a mental check. Then the eye moves to the beginning of the next point and repeats the pattern. With that in mind, look for opportunities to use bullet or numbered points. However, don't overdo it. A page full of points can look almost as tedious to read as the wall-of-words executive summary presented earlier in this chapter. Also:

- Bullet points used for no reason don't make sense.

- If you use them just because you think you should, you could confuse the reader.

- The reader will be looking for a list of instructions or recommendations where no list exists.

- That can be confusing. Enough said, yes?

Appendix One

Sample thank you note

Here is a sample thank you note, including a subject line, that was written following the W5 outline process:

Subject: Thank you for the opportunity

I wish to thank you for the confidence you have shown in me by promoting me to dispatch. I am excited about the challenges this position offers and look forward to learning as fast as I can so that I can contribute to the success of the company.

Your confidence in me is appreciated. I will work hard to meet your expectations, as this is a great opportunity.

Sincerely,
Janice Lake

Notice that the subject line conveys a clear sense of purpose. It does not just say "thank you" but it includes "the opportunity." The why, or the reason the writer is writing, is there—*thank you*—as is what the writer is thanking the reader for—*the opportunity*. When you write, look at your W5 and try to convey the most important elements in your subject line.

This repetition, restatement and elaboration, without becoming redundant, is required to achieve focus and to ensure the reader gets your message. You will see this method used in effective email messages, letters, proposals and reports. In this particular message, there is no call to action and no request for feedback, nor does the message require one.

If you are saying you could have written the thank you note without asking the W5 questions, I will not argue with you. Without asking the W5 questions, you would have written a different message—similar, perhaps but different. Also, the more complex a message is, the more important it is to ask the W5 questions before you write. In short, develop a W5 habit no matter what you want to write and you will be more likely to ask, and answer, the questions before you write important business email messages.

Sample email messages

Below are several sample email messages. Deconstruct them to see if you can find the who, what, where, when, why and/or how. Not all elements will be found in every message. Part of your job, as mentioned, is to determine what to put in and what to leave out of anything you write. Also, ask yourself the following:

- if the "why" or purpose of the email message is clear and up front

- if benefits and/or consequences (or anything else that might influence attitude) are detailed

- if the action required—if action is required—is clear

Subject: Take this snow and shovel it!

Dear Municipal Councilor Johnson,

I'm writing to resolve the issue about snow removal after a snowfall.

During the recent heavy snowfall, a few of my neighbors shoveled snow from their driveways and dumped it on city property. Unfortunately, they piled their snow at the front and back of other people's vehicles, making it difficult to exit the parking spaces.

This became a point of frustration for many of the car owners.

Would your office be able to send out notices to the residents of my neighborhood to remind them that there is a snow removal bylaw they must adhere to? If you could provide me with a response by the end of the week, it would be greatly appreciated.

Sincerely,
Sidney Smith

Subject: Sorry for missing lunch

Dear Janine,

After speaking to your husband, I realize that my absence from a recent networking lunch that we had agreed to attend upset you and I would like to apologize for missing the gathering.

There were several last minute scheduling changes at work but I should have called you. I am sorry for not doing so.

Your friendship means a great deal to me. I look forward to seeing you at lunch next month.

Sincerely,
Terri

◼ ◼ ◼

Subject: Sincerest appreciation for your help

Dear Laura,

It has been a week since I started my new job and I could not have landed the promotion without your help. I just wanted to thank you for your support. Because of your assistance, I was able to produce significant results and impress our supervisor who gave me the recommendation that opened the door to the job interview.

I would like to invite you for dinner this weekend and thank you personally. Please let me know over the next day or two if you are available. You can email or call me.

Best regards,
Sally

◼ ◼ ◼

Subject: Written Warning

It has become necessary to again remind you of your responsibilities. Since issuing a verbal warning two weeks ago, we have not seen improvements in the following areas:

- arriving at work at the scheduled time
- matching your paperwork to the product being loaded
- giving appropriate notice of non-work-related appointments

Immediate improvements in these areas are expected. They are necessary to ensure customer satisfaction. Your work-related performance will be reviewed daily.

Failure to comply with this request immediately will lead to further disciplinary action up to, and including, termination. If you have any questions, email me.

Sincerely,
Jane Lake

■ ■ ■

Subject: Overdue payment reminder

Dear Ms. Lam,

Our records indicate that payment of your account in the amount of $6,890 is 30 days overdue. A copy of invoice #181 is attached.

If the payment has been forwarded, please disregard this email. Otherwise, please submit payment by October 23.

If you are unable to submit your payment, please email or call (416) 555-1212 so that we can discuss and resolve the issue. Thank you for your cooperation.

Sincerely,
Sally Arnold

■ ■ ■

The apology email below is particularly effective. The writer explains what happened, takes full responsibility, offers the reader appropriate compensation and assures the reader it will not happen again—in three focused, concise paragraphs.

Subject: Apologies for missing Saturday's lesson

Dear Mr. Tanaka,

I would like to apologize for my scheduling mistake. During our last meeting, we decided to conduct our next training session on Saturday. I did not have my day planner with me so I could not record the date. Because we usually meet Sundays, the date slipped my mind. This does not excuse what happened and I assure you that it will not happen again.

Your time is valuable, so to compensate you for the lost time and the inconvenience there will be no charge for the next lesson.

I apologize again for my scheduling mistake and look forward to seeing you on Sunday, March 14, at 1 pm.

Regards,
George Thompson

Appendix One

Appendix Two

Hotel case study sample leads

I want to stress one last time the importance of defining your true business purpose before you write. The purpose, as you define it, directly influences the words you write, the tone you use and any action you request.

For instance, in the hotel case study, you had to write an opening paragraph to the manager of the Chelsea Hotel in London, Ontario. You had a negative experience at the hotel; however, you use the hotel on a quarterly basis because it is conveniently located and offers reasonable rates. So what is your purpose? Do you want a full or partial refund? Or do you want assurance that the problems will be fixed before you book your next business trip?

If you are angry and want a full refund, here's what you might write:

> I stayed at your hotel last week and was extremely unhappy with the service. The food was cold, the room was a mess and some of your staff members were rude. I am not at all satisfied and would like a full refund ASAP.

I am not suggesting the above passage is solidly written but it does convey a particular purpose. However, if you said that your purpose was to obtain a refund, I'd suggest you might want to think again. From the case study: "You travel to London every quarter on business. Your company has used this hotel for several years because it is conveniently located and offers reasonable rates."

With that in mind, how would you feel if you obtained a refund and the service did not improve the next time you were there? What would you have achieved? So I repeat: determine your *true* business purpose before you write. If you want assurance that the problems will be fixed before you book your next business trip, this is what you might write:

Last week I stayed at your hotel and encountered several service-related issues. Due to business in London, I had planned to stay at your hotel once a month over the next year. However, I need your assurance that service levels will improve before I commit to doing so.

In workshops, people have asked me if they can ask for assurance that conditions will improve *and* a refund. First off, what is your primary purpose? Do you want to find a new, more expensive, less conveniently located hotel? What happens if the manager grants you a refund but conditions are just as poor the next time you are there? What happens if the manager does not give you a refund?

The fact is, by asking for two things—a refund and improved conditions—you muddy the water. Instead of assuring you that conditions were improved, the manager might fight your request for a refund. That may be a sign of a poor manager but that is not your issue—not if your primary business purpose is to be assured that conditions at the hotel have improved. In short, you want to determine your true business purpose and focus on that. For instance, if you were a consumer who had stayed at the hotel in a resort area during a vacation and had experienced poor service and poor conditions, I could understand if you asked for a refund. That purpose makes sense.

For the sake of argument, let's say you disagree with the purpose I am suggesting. I have no real problem with that. In other words, if you decide that your business purpose is to obtain a refund, I am not going to say, "No, you are wrong." What I am going to say is this: Understand that you will write a different letter, based on your purpose, than I will write based on my purpose. That is the point of this exercise, to understand that purpose influences the words you use, the tone you use and the action you request.

◼ ◼ ◼

Furniture case study sample lead

Here is a possible lead for the furniture case study email:

I hope you can resolve a problem with my furniture order. On November 1, I ordered office furniture from the Office Company catalogue but two chairs were missing when my order arrived. I called to sort this out and, on November 11, I received one additional chair; however, it was the wrong color. The person I talked to about my order no longer works for you and no one seems to know about my problem. I would like you to sort this out for me by the end of the week.

I have chosen to open this email with my purpose—to get help solving the problem. Then I give some background information (because the recipient is not familiar with my problem) and end with a stronger purpose statement, one that includes a deadline.

Even though I have included a deadline, I do not spell out any consequences, such as: "I would like you to sort this out for me by the end of the week or I will return all the furniture that I have purchased at your store." If the manager does not call and assure me the problem will be sorted out, I can escalate my complaint and include consequences. By providing a deadline—the end of the week—I know that I can follow up by a specific time and escalate the complaint, if the issue is not resolved.

If you wanted to include a shorter deadline in your letter—say you needed the furniture sooner for a particular business reason—I would have no problem with that. The point is this: Before you write, you have to think about what you need, why you need it and when you need it. That way you can write a clear, concise, coherent, focused message that starts with your purpose, establishes an appropriate tone, includes relevant background information, adjusts the attitude of the reader and includes a clear and appropriate call to action.

Appendix Two

Appendix Three

Passive voice converted to active voice

The passive sentences presented in Chapter 19 have been converted to the active voice below.

More than one third of the applicants to the school failed the entrance exam.

She slammed on the brakes as the car sped downhill.

I have damaged your bicycle.

The thief damaged your bicycle.

The committee is considering action on the bill.

By then, the sound engineers will have completely remixed the soundtrack.

I wrote the paper on a computer to satisfy the instructor's demands for legibility.

The student wrote the paper on a computer to satisfy the instructor's demands for legibility.

Appendix Three

About the Author

Based in Toronto, Canada, Paul Lima has been a professional writer and writing instructor for over 25 years. He has run a successful freelance writing and business-writing training business since 1988.

For corporate clients, Paul writes media releases, promotional content, case studies, sales letters, direct-response brochures, website copy and other material

For newspapers and magazines, Paul writes about small business and technology issues. His articles have appeared in the *Globe and Mail, Toronto Star, National Post, Backbone, Profit*, CBC.ca and many other publications.

As a qualified educator, Paul conducts seminars on business writing, media interview preparation and freelance writing.

An English major from York University, Paul has worked as an advertising copywriter, continuing education manager and magazine editor.

Paul is the author of several books, listed below. Read more about him online at www.paullima.com.

Books by Paul Lima:

- *How to Write Web Copy and Social Media Content*
- *Harness the Business Writing Process*
- *Copywriting That Works: Bright ideas to Help You Inform, Persuade, Motivate and Sell!*
- *Fundamentals of Writing: How to Write Articles, Media Releases, Case Studies, Blog Posts and Social Media Content*
- *How To Write A Non-Fiction Book in 60 Days*

- *Produce, Price and Promote Your Self-Published Fiction or Non-fiction Book and eBook*

- *Everything You Wanted to Know About Freelance Writing: Find, Price, Manage Corporate Writing Assignments & Develop Article Ideas and Sell Them to Newspapers and Magazines.*

- *The Six-Figure Freelancer: How to Find, Price and Manage Corporate Writing Assignments*

- *Business of Freelance Writing: How to Develop Article Ideas and Sell Them to Newspapers and Magazines*

- *Unblock Writer's Block: How to face it, deal with it and overcome it*

- *(re)Discover the Joy of Creative Writing.*

- *How to Write Media Releases to Promote Your Business, Organization or Event*

- *Are You Ready For Your Interview? How to Prepare for Media Interviews. Prepare for interviews with print and broadcast reporters.*

- *Rebel in the Back Seat and other short stories*

Available online through www.paullima.com/books

Printed in Great Britain
by Amazon.co.uk, Ltd.,
Marston Gate.